30 ROCK
AND
PHILOSOPHY

30 ROCK
AND
PHILOSOPHY

WE WANT TO GO TO THERE

Edited by J. Jeremy Wisnewski

WILEY

John Wiley & Sons, Inc.

To pages everywhere . . .

Library of Congress Cataloging-in-Publication Data:

30 Rock and philosophy : we want to go to there / edited by J. Jeremy Wisnewski.
    p. cm.
  Includes bibliographical references and index
  ISBN 978-0-470-57558-1 (pbk.)
  1. 30 Rock (Television program) I. Wisnewsl
PN1992.77.A216A15 2010
791.45'72—dc22

Printed in the United States of America

10 9 8 7 6 5 4 3 2 1

LLYFRGELLOEDD SIR DDINBYCH	
C46 0000 0457 148	
HJ	19-Aug-2010
791.4572	£11.99
RL	

CONTENTS

PART FOUR
MIND GRAPES (TO NOURISH YOUR THINKING)

ACKNOWLEDGMENTS

Thanks for Helping Us Go to There

Television saves lives. It jumps into the lake to rescue small children, it lands aircraft in danger of crashing, it prevents natural disasters.

Okay, I'm exaggerating. But I want to thank television nonetheless. While it hasn't ended war or famine, it has provided a constant source of entertainment, and a constant occasion to bring philosophy to bear on everyday life. And for that, I can't help but be grateful.

I'm also grateful to all those folks who helped make this book possible. I've been fortunate enough to work with contributors who didn't require all of the coddling that the cast of *TGS with Tracy Jordan* needs. Thanks for getting us there, everybody! I'm also grateful to Connie Santisteban and Bill Irwin—editors who make working on topics in philosophy and pop culture as fun as it should be. Justine Gray, Nicolas Michaud, and Jackie Seamon also deserve thanks for offering feedback on the manuscript, helping open Frank's Hat Store (see Appendix 1), and collecting the wisdom of Kenneth Ellen Parcell (see Appendix 2).

Finally, I'd like to thank my wife, Dorothy Wisnewski, for the support that makes it possible for me to do everything I do. I'd also like to thank my children, Audrey and Lucian, for being as wonderful as they are.

INTRODUCTION

Platonic Fantasies and
Tina Fey-losophy

I enjoy fantasies. Not the kind you see in movies, or read about in books—the kind in my head. Since *30 Rock* debuted, I've found myself fantasizing about who the writers on the show might be. Would Plato fit in among the crowd, or Aristotle? Would Tina Fey hold her own, third-wave feminist style, against Socrates?

Aside from the small matter of being 2,400 years in the past, I can easily imagine Plato at the writers' table, lizzing away with Tina Fey as they talk through the latest script. Plato was a notorious jokester. His dialogues include jokes about self-importance (Tracy and Jenna, anyone?), jokes about incompetence (Tracy and Jenna again? Devon Banks? Kathy Geiss?), and jokes about sex (have you seen the show!?).[1] I think he'd fit right in, at least once he learned English. I can even picture his hat: Socrates Rules.

Does it seem like a bit much? Is it surprising that television can be a source for philosophical reflection? Can "real" philosophy be done in conjunction with something popular, like *30 Rock*? In asking these questions, we'd do well to remember that Plato said truth could not be written, and that he himself

1

had never written down his own philosophical teachings.[2] (I'm pretty sure Tina Fey said the same thing in some interview somewhere.) In this respect, all of Plato's dialogues can be regarded as popular writings encouraging people to come to Plato's Academy and to engage in living philosophical dialogue. The written dialogues are meant to begin the philosophical journey, not to end it. They are meant to inspire philosophical dialogue, not to replace it. This is exactly how I think of *30 Rock*, and exactly what brings me back week after week.

When I think of philosophy and *30 Rock*, I like to imagine Plato as a television writer. Plato used a popular medium of his time, the dialogue, to get people to philosophize. And I bet he would have opted for television if he lived in this century. Yes, Plato criticized imitation. Television is of course imitation— and *30 Rock* especially so—it's a show that *imitates* a show. Of course, Plato's criticism of imitation occurs in a speech given by Socrates. The speech recounts a fictional dialogue.[3] Plato was certainly aware that a speech about a dialogue was only an imitation of a dialogue, much as Tina Fey is aware that *TGS* isn't a real show. One can't help but imagine Plato smiling about what he'd done. If he were a television writer, we'd expect no less: he would surely criticize the crap that's on television in whatever show he was writing.

And yes, I like to think of Tina Fey and the writers of *30 Rock* as a collective modern-day Plato (I said I enjoyed fantasy!). They put in just enough shenanigans (to use a little Irish slang) to keep viewers entranced. What does it mean to be black or white? What does it mean to live the good life? Should moral rules always be followed? Can Frank really be gay for just one guy? What is the nature of friendship? How can we know anything at all about the world? These questions arise on the set of *TGS*—and they persist.

Kenneth says he loves two things: everybody and television. While I can't honestly say I love everyone, I concur whole-heartedly with Kenneth on television. It is a glorious invention, and a remarkable source of wonder. Where else can we view worlds that do not exist, full of quirky characters, doing endlessly amusing things? Where else can we find Tracy Jordon calling Colorado a "white myth," Jack Donaghy admitting that he has a cookie jar collection, and Liz Lemon flashing a breast? And when we get to a television show *about* a television show, well, that's nearly too good to be true.

Aristotle claimed that philosophy begins in wonder, so it's no surprise that philosophy can arise from watching television—especially when the show is about television, and full of some of the silliest stuff imaginable. Wonder is one of the benefits of watching *30 Rock*, and philosophy can't help but be there too, bubbling up and spilling over everything.

NOTES

1. Many of Plato's early dialogues poke fun at both incompetence and self-importance. "Euthyphro," for example, is about a fellow who thinks he knows what morality is, and even claims to be able to see the future. Of course, the future he sees involves Socrates being acquitted at his trial—which obviously is *not* what happens (Socrates is sentenced to death). The name "Euthyphro" itself can be roughly translated as "straight-thinker"—an obvious snicker at this arrogant SOB. In *The Republic*, as elsewhere, Plato makes his fair share of sex jokes—not the least of which is about women training in the nude, riding "studs" just like men (and yes, all the sexual connotations are there in the Greek, too).

2. See "Phaedrus" and Plato's Seventh Letter. For a wonderful defense of this view of Plato's writings, see James Arieti's *Interpreting Plato: The Dialogues as Drama* (Savage, MD: Rowman and Littlefield Publishers, 1991).

3. The text is *The Republic*. It begins with Socrates recalling a conversation. We have no idea who he's talking to—he just jumps right in. This makes the book already an imitation of dialogue, since Socrates (Plato's mouthpiece) is the only speaker in the whole of *The Republic* (when he reports what others say, after all, it's still him doing the talking). A second layer of imitation is present in the very fact that the reported dialogue is *written*, rather than spoken. In this sense, *The Republic* is twice removed from actual dialogue: it is a written, and hence doesn't have the give-and-take of dialogue, and it's presented in a speech by Socrates (so there's only one person talking). Plato knew what he was doing—namely, messing with his readers!

PART ONE

WHAT WOULD OPRAH DO?: ETHICS AND THE GOOD LIFE AT *30 ROCK*

BEING KENNETH: SOME MORAL LESSONS

P. Sue Dohnimm[1]

Kenneth makes my heart skip. It isn't his dashing good looks or his wonderful sense of style. It isn't just the endearing fact that his middle name is Ellen. Honestly, it's the simplicity of his moral vision. He just sees the world in a way that I can't even imagine. It's an enchanted world, where right and wrong are as plain as the pee and laughter combination we call lizzing. I have the same question Jack Donaghy has.

> Jack: Kenneth, I wonder what it's like seeing the world through your eyes?
>
> Kenneth: I don't know, Mr. Donaghy. Well, I think I see the world pretty much the same as everyone else.
>
> Jack: Really? [*music starts, Jack continues, singing*] 'Cause I think you're very special, Kenneth [*Jack is now seen through Kenneth's eyes, as a puppet.*], to be able to get so much joy from simple things, simple things. . . .

Jack [*talking again, and human*]: But most of us grow up and lose our sense of wonder. ["Apollo, Apollo"]

Kenneth sees things uniquely. He is literal-minded. When Jack says, "Now look at me," after talking about some of the things he went through as a child, Kenneth simply says, "I already did" ("Apollo, Apollo"). Kenneth is thrilled with a key-chain he got on his last birthday, joyous because "every time you move his head, his head moves! Look!"

The disenchanted world is complicated. The decisions we have to make can make us unsure of ourselves. We face challenges of all kinds. We're befuddled by moral dilemmas in which we have to make difficult choices. Do we let Jenna fall as she plays Peter Pan in order to get back at her for sleeping with Dennis? Do we let Frank go to law school given his family history? Do we call the ambulance right away when we hit Mom with the car? Kenneth doesn't seem to be bothered by such dilemmas. He sees the world with absolute clarity. There's only right and wrong.

Kenneth's Moral Universe

Jack sees the world in terms of dollar signs. Tracy sees the world egocentrically—everyone is just another Tracy Jordan, having no interests other than Tracy's.

Kenneth lives in a different world. His moral universe involves following a moral code no matter how difficult it is. It's a world where lying is wrong, where one must never steal, and where doing good for others is paramount. Kenneth's good deeds are all over *30 Rock*. Whether he's accompanying Liz Lemon to recover her phone from an unscrupulous cabby, or swearing his undying love for television, Kenneth seems to emit moral virtue like it's going out of style (and maybe it is). When Tracy disappears to save himself from the wrath of the Black Crusaders, Kenneth knows his whereabouts, but refuses to break his vow to Tracy ("Hiatus"). Liz and Jack yell at him, threaten him, call him a "mouth-breathing Appalachian," but it's to no avail. His promise stands strong. When Tracy is running late to *TGS*, Kenneth sacrifices his body to get Tracy there on time. Kenneth voluntarily falls down some concrete stairs so that Tracy can use the ambulance to get him to the show on time (ambulances are only for real emergencies, after all) ("Hiatus"). When Kenneth wins Pete's wedding ring in a game of poker, he simply gives it back. He can't see his way clear to keeping it ("Blind Date").

These acts of kindness and principle seem to make Kenneth what we might call a "rule absolutist." For the rule absolutist, the moral law dictates what's appropriate, and it's appropriate *everywhere and always*. There are no exceptions to moral rules. Period. Immanuel Kant (1724–1804) is the philosopher usually associated with this view, though perhaps a little unfairly. For Kant, morality demands absolute consistency in action. It involves never making an exception of oneself, and always holding oneself to the highest moral standard. The rule is everything for the rule absolutist.

By contrast, one might think of moral rules as useful guidelines for navigating the difficult waters of everyday life. These rules, however, need to occasionally be set aside when the circumstances demand it. Of course, it's easy to be wrong about what the circumstances demand, so one shouldn't set aside rules lightly. All the same, there will be some cases where a rule like "never lie" will lead us astray. (When the Nazis ask if we're hiding any Jews, saying "Yes, they're upstairs" would arguably *not* be an example of moral action! And the same goes for telling the Black Crusaders where Tracy is.) With this view, morality is a *context-specific* affair. We can call this *contextual absolutism*. The most famous advocate of this kind of view is Aristotle (384–322 BCE).

As the name indicates, this conception of morality doesn't equate to any kind of *moral antirealism*—the view that *there are no* moral truths. The idea, rather, is that there *is* always a right thing to do, it's just that rules can't tell us in advance what that thing will be. We have to pay special attention to the circumstances of our action, and act accordingly. The moral sage is the person who always *sees* all of the relevant features of a given situation, and responds to them appropriately. In this respect, the moral sage has no need for rules. Rules might help us to reach a stage where we act morally most of the time, but they're only a ladder that we must climb up. Once we've attained moral wisdom, the ladder itself can be discarded.[2]

Kenneth certainly believes that there's a singular right thing to do. But is he a rule absolutist? Does he take his moral rules so seriously that he simply can't set them aside? In a surprising number of cases, Kenneth does set specific rules aside—and he sometimes does so for all the wrong reasons. But in a complicated world like New York City, what's the son of a pig farmer from Stone Mountain to do?

Tested Virtue

Kenneth doesn't seem to fetishize rules. He doesn't seem to hold to them in all circumstances no matter what, valuing them in themselves. For example, when Tracy and his wife, Angie, are on the verge of breaking up for good, Kenneth sets aside his aversion to deception. He tries to intervene. By pretending to be interested in Angie as a sexual partner in an attempt to make Tracy jealous, Kenneth Ellen Parcell claims he's real good at the sexy stuff, and that he'd like to visit Angie "at night." We know he doesn't mean it, and we know why he's doing it. He wants to trick Tracy, to *deceive* him.

Kenneth attempts the same kind of deception when Tracy doesn't take his risk of diabetes seriously. He constructs an elaborate ruse involving a story he first heard from his Mee-Maw: the Hill Witch torments those who don't eat their vegetables! In an effort to get Tracy to eat right, Kenneth pretends to be the Hill Witch, trying to scare Tracy into a healthy lifestyle (ultimately, it's Jenna who manages to successfully impersonate the Hill Witch).

So maybe Kenneth isn't a rule absolutist: he's willing to engage in deception for a greater good. But the strategy can backfire. Consider, for instance, when Tracy tells Kenneth to "pleasure" his wife as a way of making up for Tracy's (pretend) infidelities. When Tracy rushes to stop the consummation, he finds Kenneth looking pale, eating a sandwich, sitting next to Grizz.

> Tracy [*running into his house*]: I'm going to kill you, Kenneth the Page!

> Kenneth: I'm sorry, Mr. Jordan. I just couldn't do it.

> Angie: This boy comes to the door, tries to kiss me, then he throws up, and starts crying.

> Kenneth: My body wouldn't let me violate the sacred bonds of marriage, sir.

Kenneth's ability to bend the moral rules has its limits. While Kenneth might be able to be set aside some moral rules briefly (like not deceiving others), he can't set them aside easily— and certainly not for long. When Kenneth tries to get Tracy to believe he's hitting on Angie, for example, he stutters through his pickup lines, using every cliché he can think of. When the ruse is complete, he has trouble taking a drink from his bottled water, shaken by his venture into rule-breaking.

Kenneth's willingness to set aside a moral rule may well indicate that he's a contextual absolutist—that is, he may think that morality sometimes requires setting aside our usual roles. But there's some evidence to the contrary here as well. While Liz is right to call Kenneth a "sweet kid," he doesn't always seem so sweet—particularly when he's doing something for someone else (like Jack).

> Jack: The only reason I sent you to Banks was to get information. Why were you telling him anything?

Kenneth: I'm sorry, sir. I had to keep talking just to stop him from putting his fingers in my mouth.

Jack: Kenneth, you are the worst gay bait ever.

Kenneth [*upset*]: You used me?

Jack: For television. Kenneth, I humiliated you for television.

Kenneth [*excited*]: Like on *What's Happening?*, when that man used Re-run to bootleg that Doobie Brothers concert!

Jack: Exactly. And I need to humiliate you again. I've got a very important meeting coming up and Banks cannot be there.

Kenneth: And you want me to kill him . . .

Jack: No. I want you to distract him. You've got to make sure he doesn't leave that hotel room tomorrow morning.

Kenneth: I'll do it. Just like Sydney Bristow on *Alias*, I'll use my sexuality as a weapon. To the wig shop! [*runs away, smiling*]. ["Fireworks"]

And this is certainly not the only time Kenneth is asked to use his sexual energy as a trap for Devon Banks. It's also not the only time he decides to actively deceive others. Television is hardly the greater good, even though Kenneth most certainly thinks it is. Do these examples show that Kenneth isn't the moral beacon we thought he was? Perhaps. Or perhaps not.

There's another way of understanding Kenneth's moral lapses—and one that fits perfectly with Kenneth's personality. Kenneth's immoral actions all stem from the same unholy trinity: gullibility, trust, and unflappable loyalty. He sets aside rules for the greater good, but he also sets aside rules when he thinks he's serving a higher cause (like television, or his friendship with Liz). He's no moral sage, to be sure. He lacks the wisdom for that. As Frank puts it in describing why Kenneth's so good at poker, "He's awesome. You can't read his thoughts because he doesn't have any" ("Blind Date").

The simplicity of Kenneth's moral vision is thus also Kenneth's downfall. He's too easily duped into giving up parts of his moral vision by his trust in and loyalty to others. This is a central danger of seeing the world through Kenneth's eyes: it is a beautiful world full of happiness and song, but also a world where we can be led to act against our own principles.

Olympic Tetherball: A Final Lesson on Moral Frailty

After learning that many of his most beloved Olympic events were faked to improve ratings, Kenneth has a sit-down with Jack.

Kenneth: "Believe in the stars". . . it's like that doesn't even mean anything anymore.

Jack: Kenneth, I'm sure I can trust your discretion about what happened in my office today. What you overheard was some rather grown-up talk.

Kenneth: Was any of it real, Mr. Donaghy? Beer pong? Jazzercise? Women's soccer?

Jack: You're not in Stone Mountain anymore, Kenneth. This is the real world, and not everything is in black and white.

Kenneth: There's always a right thing to do, Mr. Donaghy. Just sometimes, it's not the easy thing to do. [*gets up*] Tyler Brody was not the only hero I lost today. [*Kenneth begins to walk away, but stops and turns back.*] The other hero was you, in case that—

Jack [*interrupts*]: I got it, Kenneth. ["Believe in the Stars"]

Kenneth's reaction to Jack promotes a pang of conscience in Jack. For all of Kenneth's hillbilly moral sentiment—for all that he fails to see in the world—his vision of the good acts as a reminder of how the world *could* be. Jack later worries that somebody "would have to be a complete monster to lose his respect." This leads him to try to convince Kenneth that a person can be good even when that person chooses to violate some moral rules without appealing to any greater good.

Jack: Kenneth, I'm a good person.

Kenneth: If you say so, sir.

Jack: But sometimes life is complicated. There isn't always a right answer. Say you're on a lifeboat.

Kenneth: You're on a lifeboat.

Jack: The boat holds eight people, but you have nine on board. Either you will capsize, and everyone will drown, or one person can be sacrificed to save the others. Now, how do you decide who should die?

Kenneth: Oh, I don't believe in hypothetical situations, Mr. Donaghy. That's like lying to your brain.

Jack: Kenneth, you've lived a sheltered life. Virtue never tested is no virtue at all.

Kenneth: Oh, I have been tested, sir. There are only two things I love in this world: everybody, and television. But up in my neighborhood we can't even afford cable. So my neighbor the Colonel and I just watch whatever the old rabbit-ears will pick up. A lot of folks have chosen to go ahead and steal cable from the poor, defenseless cable company. But not me. As bad as I want all of those channels, I don't do it because stealing is wrong!

Jack: Kenneth, I'm familiar with the Ten Commandments.

Kenneth: Ten?

When Jack tries to test Kenneth's virtue in an elevator (telling him they're stuck there, and that someone must die), Kenneth opts to make *himself* the victim. Not to be outstripped, Jack tries to test Kenneth's moral mettle in another way. He sets up illegal cable in Kenneth's apartment, along with a new flat-screen TV. Kenneth is visibly ashamed the next day, having watched the stolen delight that is cable television.

Jack: Did you have a good night, Kenneth?

Kenneth: Oh yes, sir. Hardly any screaming from the Colonel. Actually I was thinking . . . we all try to be perfect, but the world may be, well . . . uh, what I'm trying to say is that . . . there's a whole channel on the cable that just tells you what's on the other channels . . .

Jack: I know, Kenneth, it's okay.

We all make mistakes sometimes. Morality is harder than many of us think. When we err, we should face our failure with resolve, not with shame. And this might be the central lesson that we can learn from Kenneth Ellen Parcell.

Besides, as Kenneth reminds us, "Everybody knows that the only thing we should be ashamed of is our bodies" ("Succession").

NOTES

1. The "P" is still silent.

2. This metaphor is most famously used by Ludwig Wittgenstein (1989–1951), though he was by no means the first. The same metaphor can be found in ancient China as well, in Chuang-Tzu (fourth century BCE), for example.

SOUR LEMON: LIZ'S WORKAHOLISM AND THE MEANING OF LIFE

Jeffrey A. Hinzmann

As her name suggests, Liz Lemon is a somewhat unhappy, bitter person. Though Liz has her good qualities—her sense of humor, uniqueness, and moments of self-deluded optimism—she is also irritable, moody, and *always* overworked. Being overworked, incidentally, is a key factor in her constellation of otherwise unrelated complaints. Liz can never seem to exercise, eat right, look right, write right, find Mr. Right, or even have more than a moment to herself; and work seems to be the underlying factor. Indeed, Liz complains constantly about work, both the amount of it she does and about the craziness of her coworkers. It's hard to even imagine her dropping the subject.

Add to this her boss Jack Donaghy, who tries to take her under his wing and make her both a professional *and* a personal success. Jack thinks that Liz can be both (presumably because he sees himself as both), but perhaps the facts about Liz will tell us more. Specifically, I think that a look at how work rules Liz's life can best be explained by the ideas of Karl Marx (1818–1883) and his successors. Marx is one of the great original theorists of work, and one of the first to show us how it can shape much of our destinies. Before reporting me to the updated House Un-American Activities Committee, though, let me make my case: starting, appropriately enough, with a look at Liz's life itself.

Blerg! Nerds! And Other Liz Lemon–Droppings

What is Liz Lemon's life like exactly? She's the head writer for *The Girlie Show* (*TGS*), a live variety and sketch show strangely similar to *Saturday Night Live.* (In case it's hard to connect the dots, try to remember that actress Tina Fey originally attained her fame from her time on *SNL*. So *TGS* is probably supposed to be a thinly disguised stand-in for it). While *TGS* is a madcap show where the audience expects the unexpected, it seems that this is less the product of artifice than the simple continuation of how things go behind the scenes. In other words, *TGS* is a crazy show, starring some crazy people—Jenna Maroney and Tracy Jordan chief among them—and keeping it all together really taxes Liz's energy. But this is not all. The writers and other staff members are just crazy enough to give Jenna and Tracy a run for their money, meaning Liz has little help in keeping *TGS* under control.

Considering what's normal for her workplace, Liz is something of an oddity; she eschews style for substance, and recklessness for responsibility. Her determination to rein in all this craziness keeps *TGS* running as well as it does—which is not especially well. Add to this the constant stream of equally strange schemes and instructions from Jack Donaghy's office on high, and the tragicomedic barrenness of Liz's personal life, and we begin to see that Liz Lemon is a human fault line, pressured on all sides and ready to snap at any moment.

In truth, Liz snaps constantly. Her minor but nonetheless significant breakdowns are often central themes of whole episodes. These minor breakdowns, however, are of a piece with the madcap atmosphere that almost passes for normalcy at 30 Rockefeller Plaza. Thus, Liz is not especially notice-able as a stressed-out person. She is, however, much more committed to her job than most of her coworkers are. Tracy and Jenna are particularly indifferent to *TGS* as an institu-tion, absorbed as they are in their own personal realities. As long as they can be famous, they don't seem to care where they work. The writers, similarly, prefer writing in general to writing for *TGS* in particular—Frank being the notable exception. Jack Donaghy is in charge of *TGS*, but he's also in charge of many other business ventures as an executive of the mongrel corporation NBC-Universal-Shinehardt Wig Company: he too isn't very invested in the continued exis-tence of *TGS*. Only Liz, and to a lesser extent the hyper-loyal simpleton Kenneth the Page are really concerned to keep *TGS* running. What's less clear, however, is exactly what drives Liz to be so invested in running *TGS*, and why she sacrifices so much for it.

What has she sacrificed? For starters, we can look to all the patronizing advice Liz constantly receives from her so-called friends, mainly Jenna and Jack. Both are constantly trying to tell her how to improve her life, particularly in regard to dating and preserving what's left of her femininity. Liz isn't unattractive, but she clearly suffers from low self-esteem due, in part, to her inability to spend much time exercising or beautifying herself. She's worn down by the constant suggestions that she isn't feminine enough, isn't pretty enough, and isn't motivated enough to find a decent man. Liz, for example, is accused of being a lesbian because of her taste in shoes, which she rather obviously wears for comfort due to her constant exhaustion. Not surprisingly, Liz sees her search for a man as a desperate and doomed struggle in which she would be lucky to meet anyone up to her standards. More often than not, Liz is seen as interested in men who are out of her league.

The episode "The Ones," for example, opens in a jewelry store where Liz is helping Jack pick out an engagement ring for his girlfriend Elisa (played by Selma Hayek). When the jewelry store salesman hears Jack ask to buy a ring, he first takes a quick look at Liz and asks Jack, "Are you sure?" He then tries to humor what he believes to be Jack's poor taste in brides with the patronizing quip, "She's very spirited, like a show horse. You're a lucky man." Jack catches on to the salesman's misunderstanding and explains that he is not engaged to Liz. He then produces a picture of Elisa, and receives an expression of congratulations that is both sincere (since Elisa is assumed to be a much better catch than Liz) and relieved (because the salesman no longer has to puzzle over why a man as apparently successful and important as Jack would possibly be with Liz, not to mention that he no longer has to humor Jack). Jack is then shown the "real" rings, instead of the phony ones shown to losers (or the men buying rings for them). Though the scene is extremely brief (barely more than a minute), it encapsulates how Liz is perceived and treated by friends and strangers alike.

As if this didn't paint a bleak enough picture of Liz's life, we can see more clearly how dire her dating situation is by noting that her most serious relationship thus far (that we know of) has been to Dennis Duffy, an unquestioned loser. Dennis is the self-proclaimed "beeper king" of New York City (with the understanding that beepers are an obsolete, if not antiquated, technology), a world-class mooch (he lived off Liz's income for much of their relationship), and a sex addict who slept with Jenna opportunistically. As if these weren't serious enough indictments of Dennis, he was also caught on *Dateline NBC*'s segment "To Catch a Predator" attempting to have sex with an underage girl he "was sure was twenty-two" even though she said she was sixteen. As of this writing, Dennis was last seen trying to rebuild himself by investing in a basement vending machine, oblivious to how little income it's likely to bring him. For all of this, however, Liz has spent seasons of the show struggling to not just settle for Dennis. The main things Dennis had to offer Liz were acceptance of her quirks and his understanding of her love of food. Even Jenna and Jack think she can do better—some small encouragement for Liz at least.

Sadly, Liz is unable to maintain a promising relationship with Floyd because of his transfer to Cleveland. At a key juncture in their relationship, Liz contemplates moving to Cleveland with Floyd, and travels there with him to see what she would think of the move. The visit shows her a glimpse of a personal heaven. Liz is stopped on the street and asked if she's a model and then implored to eat because she's "so skinny." She's greeted by police officers who ask her to pet their horse (rather than aggressively search her as in New York). She has a blast at the Rock & Roll Hall of Fame, she could live like a queen if she stayed with Floyd (who can afford a swanky house in Cleveland), and last but certainly not least, she is spontaneously offered a job as the hostess of a cooking show simply on the basis of her attractiveness and TV experience. In other words, Liz would be treated with dramatically more respect, she would be seen as feminine and beautiful, and she wouldn't be nearly as stressed-out as in New York. In spite of all these potential benefits of changing location (not to mention being able to stay with Floyd), she passes it all up because she can't leave *TGS* and New York. While it's not clear why Liz is so attached to her job at this point, we get a pretty good clue from the episode "Jackie Jormp-Jomp."

Sources of the Sour Self

"Jackie Jormp-Jomp" opens with Liz on involuntary leave, the target of a sexual harassment complaint for her attempted quid pro quo of sexual favors for her employees' jobs. She sneaks back to work briefly (in violation of her probation) and when caught, gets sympathy from Jack, who says, "People like us, we need the stress, we're only happy when we're overcoming obstacles." In the meantime, she fills the time by chatting up the doormen at her building, completely oblivious to how sick they are of her (she insists, at her self-deluded best, that "I brighten their day"). Following one of these "conversations," she has a chance meeting with Emily, a woman in her building. Emily quickly guesses Liz's situation, and before long, explains Liz's relationship to work with remarkable succinctness. She tells Liz, "You get addicted to the stress, think it gives your life purpose." Let's see if she's right.

Emily invites Liz to hang out with her friends, baiting her with the claim that "it just takes time to realize there are much better ways to be happy." Liz is intrigued enough to give this group a try, but not so convinced that she has managed to shut up about work. Instead, she reluctantly joins Emily and her friends (a group of women who have colorful stories about how they became independently wealthy), while they drink, shop, dine, and pamper themselves. Liz gradually comes to enjoy this lifestyle so much that she sexually harasses her sexual harassment counselor (at her reinstatement hearing, no less!) in order to return to her probation and continue to enjoy her life of leisure with Emily and her new friends. Liz knows she cannot afford to be out of work forever, but reveals to a concerned Jack that she has enough saved up to not work for "two years, maybe four if I give up cable . . . so I'll be back to the show in four years." Jack is, as usual, a surprisingly good friend to Liz, explaining that "you're fooling yourself, you know you can't live like that," and prophetically adding that "there is no solace in their luxury, only deep despair."

Liz, of course, does not want to believe Jack's warning. In fact, she's so determined to prove him wrong that she repeats his assessment to Emily and company later that night, and is surprised to hear Emily respond by saying, "Actually, that's true." One of Emily's friends, a former neurosurgeon, explains that "the human brain needs stimulation, or it atrophies and your pleasure center literally shrinks. That's why we do our 'special activity' to combat that." The "special activity" turns out to be an underground fight club. Emily's neurosurgeon friend insists that "the pain *proves* we're alive" while Emily baits her into a fight. Liz responds that "this is *very* disappointing," partly because her alternative to work didn't pan out, and presumably because once again she must acknowledge that Jack was right. When Liz attempts to refuse and simply leave, the ladies inform her that she'll have to fight her way out. We next see her, black-eyed, cut, and bruised, letting Jack know that he was right. He nonchalantly asks, "What did they turn out to be, lesbians?" Liz replies, "No, fight club," while pointing to her black eye with equal nonchalance. The episode ends with Liz admonishing a puzzled Jenna and Tracy for their latest screwup. They are puzzled because Liz is positively beaming with joy while doing it, even though the situation calls for real anger on her part. She's smiling because she finally appreciates the meaning that her job (which consists largely of putting out fires, solving ridiculous interpersonal conflicts, and yes, babysitting Jenna and Tracy) brings to her life. Liz is happy again— at least as happy as she can be while still working at *TGS*.

Liz is trapped in a paradoxical situation that affects many working Americans; the meaning of her life comes from her work, which is so demanding of her time that she cannot pursue any of the other things usually regarded as meaningful. Now we understand why Liz spends her free nights at home "working on the night cheese," why she found Dennis so appealing to stay with and Floyd so hard to commit to, and why she spent most of season two trying to convince adoption officials that she would be a minimally competent mother. She just can't really contemplate leaving her job. Sigmund Freud (1856–1939) famously said that people need two things to be happy, "work and love." Liz, like many Americans, is pushed into the awkward choice of either work *or* love, rather than having a realistic chance of having both. Liz's workaholism is a preference for what seems increasingly to be the more stable of the two options.

Work, Love, and Marxism

When you hear the word "Marxism" nowadays, it's usually associated with some other political dirty words, like "communism" and "socialism." These are words we all know, because our parents were raised to hate and fear them. Even I remember being taught, as a wee lad, to constantly fear that the Soviet Union would nuke the world; the thought scared the crap out of me until I realized that elementary school was enough to worry about. Nonetheless, these kinds of attitudes have created some serious misunderstandings about the philosophical contributions of Karl Marx. While hardly anyone defends Marx's vision of a utopia with no social classes, especially following the collapse of many of the world's communist societies, many people still find his vision inspiring (when we see a classless society on *Star Trek*, we don't get so freaked out).[1]

Additionally, we are able to appreciate the moral concerns that prompted Marx to criticize capitalism and put the idea of an alternative form of society in people's minds. Marx's main concern was with the unjust exploitation of workers, which resulted in feelings of alienation. Liz is definitely a member of the bourgeoisie (the social upper class—think white-collar jobs and successful entrepreneurs). Members of this class are usually seen as the exploiters of the proletariat (the labor or lower class—in today's terms think of anything minimum-wage and blue-collar). Liz is far from exploiting her workers. As her suspension for sexual harassment reveals, she's a very fair and caring boss, willing to go the distance to help her employees. Furthermore, the other members of *TGS* are also bourgeois.[2]

Liz is exploited and alienated, but not in exactly the ways Marx described. Marx's theories were formed to explain the economy of the Victorian-era industrial revolution, and are therefore somewhat out of date. Marx assumed that alienation was the result of not being in control of one's work (alienated labor), as exemplified by the kinds of brutal, mindless jobs that were common in factories. In jobs such as these, one employee is the same as another, no one is special. While such a concern still applies to cubicle slaves depicted in the comic strip "Dilbert" and the movie *Office Space*, it does not describe Liz. She has a creative job and lots of freedom to write the kinds of material she wants. Of course she must cater to what her boss asks of her and what the audience wants, but her job involves much less alienation from her labor than most jobs in society.

Instead, Liz is socially and *existentially* alienated, unable to feel normal or connect with people around her. This, in turn, is the reason all the other characters on the show are convinced she is so odd. This doesn't mean that Marxism isn't relevant here, however. In fact, Marx's successors developed a more sophisticated grasp of how capitalism exploits workers, creates social and existential alienation, and traps people in life situations from which escape is nearly impossible. Liz might, in her own way, be as trapped working for *TGS* as Oliver Twist was in his life of poverty. Liz allows NBC-Universal-Shinehardt to have her at their beck and call for the best years of her life. She is never seriously tempted away from work by the promise of love, or driven away by exhaustion.

The German critical theorist Theodor Adorno (1903–1969) led a group of Marxist thinkers known as the Frankfurt School (so named because they were originally based out of the School for Social Research in Frankfurt, Germany) in trying to improve Marxism by explaining how people are the victims of social manipulation the likes of which they cannot fully understand. Of central importance to their modernized Marxism was the question of why the workers never saw themselves as oppressed. To do this, the Frankfurt School combined Marx's study of social class with Freud's psychology to account for the subtleties of an individual's development. Adorno thought the problem was that people could be easily misdirected. Rather than look at the true nature of their situation, people are subtly encouraged to turn a blind eye to the ways their lives have been shaped by the social structures of their times. This misdirection is the result of *ideology*, another concept coined by Marx. Ideologies are views (including philosophical theories) that seem to be unbiased, rational accounts of lofty ideas, but in fact boil down to justifications of the status quo.

According to Marxism, the most pernicious ideologies are those that support capitalism, such as meritocracy and free will. Views like these encourage people to continue to see themselves as creators of their own destiny regardless of mitigating circumstances. As a result, people blame themselves for their failure to rise to fame and fortune, and they overlook how unlikely they were to succeed playing a rigged game. The most obvious comparison is with gambling at a casino. The individual is free to play or not to play, but the saying "The house always wins" indicates that the game is set up so that the player is far more likely to lose than win. The ideology in this analogy would be the belief that the outcome of the game is mostly chance and therefore that the gambler has a reasonable chance of winning. The critical theorists were inclined to see the free market in a similar way; the apparent choices and freedoms offered by our society are actually just there to pay lip service to the people's beliefs, but behind-the-scenes manipulations do much to guarantee the stability of the upper-class. This indicates an important dis-analogy between the casino and the market; the individual is free to stop gambling regardless of how fair or unfair it might be, but the economic market is pervasive and there are few, if any, viable alternatives to participating in it in order to survive in modern society. This makes the upper-class's hold on the market all the more pernicious.

Marx can't tell us everything we need to know about Liz's workaholism, but his successors, following the path he started, are able to complete the picture. The picture is this: Liz is mainly seen as a worker by NBC-Universal-Shinehardt. As a worker, Liz is worked as much as possible, with little regard to the consequences to the rest of her life. Even though Jack, her boss, sees her as a person, he does not seem to realize his role in the conflict. Instead, he gives Liz advice about how to better make use of her time while not at work. Jack fails, however, to realize that working as much as Liz does, it's difficult for Liz to invest emotionally in anything outside of the job. Indeed, Jack's failure to appreciate Liz's situation probably has a lot to do with his own level of privilege. He's paid so much money (and given so many perks) that he finds it easier to strike a proper balance between work and love. Like Liz, though, his life primarily revolves around work, thus ensuring that he will never advise Liz to take time off work.

When Life Gives You Liz's Lemons, Can You Make Lemonade?

After this parade of cynical thinkers and their views, one might feel that we've lost sight of Liz Lemon's problems and have also possibly lost any sense of hope for the future. I'll at least try to clear up how this applies to Liz, but you're on your own to find hope for yourself. Perhaps, though, if I can convince you that Liz's case isn't hopeless, you won't think things are so bad. So bear with me.

Liz has tried her best to live a rich, meaningful life with places for both work and love. She seems stuck, however, in the unfortunate position of choosing between one and the other. As Adorno and the critical theorists would have predicted, though, Liz has trouble seeing her job as the problem. Worse still, on those rare moments when she does seem to realize that work might be part of the problem, her own dependence on it as a source of meaning makes it all the harder for her to get the distance that she needs to get clear on her priorities and make really good choices for herself. In the future, Liz will probably cling desperately to her job as her hopes for a husband and family get ever more remote. Her friendship with Jack might well be like having a substitute husband, while Jenna and Tracy are essentially playing the role of her children. But is this the final word on the matter? Is there anything Liz can really do about it?

Even though Liz can't quite see the maze she's in, and finds solace in running around the maze with extra energy like a spunky lab rat, she can still eventually find her way out. It's always possible that she'll luck out, and wind up in a relationship that works with her oppressive work schedule. More significantly, Liz can accept responsibility for getting what she really wants out of life. This is a good first step, but it's hardly enough. Liz will also have to figure out whether she really wants anything that will possibly pull her away from *TGS* (doesn't seem like it), and whether she might be willing to put some distance between herself and *TGS* to make some of her other dreams come true. She almost did in "Jackie Jormp-Jomp," but she had the bad luck of stumbling on an alternative even worse than work. Perhaps if she tried it again, older and wiser, things might go better the second time around. If she doesn't find love, she might at least become a contender in her local fight club.

NOTES

1. Understanding how a vision could be inspiring but not widely defended is no more problematic that understanding why a religion might be appealing if one is not inclined to take it literally. I can find the idea of heaven inspiring, even if I am not a Christian.

2. The one exception here is likely to be Kenneth the Page, whom Jack describes as the socioeconomic equivalent of an "inner-city Latina woman." Given our common correlations between race, neighborhood, and socioeconomic level, he's saying Kenneth is right above the poverty line.

FRIENDSHIP ON *30 ROCK*: WHAT A GREEK PHILOSOPHER CAN TEACH US ABOUT COMPANIONSHIP

Dan Yim

I run with a crowd that loves *30 Rock*. So it should come as no surprise that we unwind from the workweek by talking about *30 Rock* and tossing back a few drinks. Picture the following scene: an artist, two middle-school teachers, a belly dancer, a financial planner, a couple of college professors, and a construction worker huddled around a pub table downtown talking about the show.

An outsider might wonder why this sitcom inspires such seriously fun discussion among people who are so different in their day jobs, personalities, and value commitments. The answer, quite simply, is that we're all human, and *30 Rock* is more than *just* a hilarious popular television comedy. *30 Rock* deals with some deep issues of human life, such as what it means to be a good person and what things in life are *truly* valuable. Human life is often deeply serious and comedic *at the same time.*

Take for instance how much we value our friends. The best and worst of our human experiences come from how healthy or sick our friendships are. Friendship is serious business, and it's never trivial to ask whether our relationships are going well. The way that we obsess over some of our relationships, however, can be hilarious. How many of us have worried that so-and-so hasn't called? We go temporarily insane spinning into conspiracy theory mode, only to find out that the reason they didn't call is innocent—they misplaced their cell phone or something like that. That's funny, but it also shows how much we value the way that our friendships are growing and evolving. *30 Rock* combines the serious with the hilarious in ways that speak to all of us, no matter how different we are in our life experiences, jobs, or values. That's why it can unite a group that consists of a belly dancer and a college professor, two personalities that you might not put at the same table.

When my happy hour group talks about *30 Rock*, it's almost always about the characters and their relationships. Our latest discussion involved a disagreement about Liz Lemon. Her closest friend is Jenna Maroney, or so you might think. Some of us were perplexed about what it means to be a close friend, much less a friend at all. It's strange, isn't it—when you start asking really basic questions about something as familiar as friendship, it becomes puzzling. Does friendship require that you've known this person for a really long time? Does it require that you've made sacrifices for this person? Does it require that you've been through bad times as well as good times together? We found it hard to answer these questions. The disagreement got even more complicated when we started talking about Jack Donaghy and his relationship with Liz Lemon. Between those pairs—Liz/Jenna and Liz/Jack—who has the better friendship? That of course got us talking about the status of all the relationships among the main characters. We argued about Tracy

Jordan's relationship with his ridiculously loyal entourage of Grizz and Dot Com. How about the occasional odd alliance between Tracy and Jenna? Are they friends? What does it even mean to be "friends"? Well, this is what sometimes happens when a conversation gets philosophical.

I'm sad to say that our conversation went nowhere, partly because we were on our fourth round of drinks, but mostly because we skipped a crucial step: coming up with common criteria and definitions of friendship. We decided to settle this debate and to talk about the main characters' relationships at the next happy hour.

Aristotle to the Rescue

When the next Friday rolled around, I brought some help. I decided to enlist the aid of a guy named Aristotle (384–322 BCE), a philosopher of ancient Greece. He was the protégé of another philosopher named Plato (ca. 428–348 BCE), and he eventually became the private tutor of the Greek conqueror Alexander the Great. One of Aristotle's best-known writings is the *Nicomachean Ethics*, in which he gives an outline of the things that go into a well-lived human life. One of the critical ingredients is friendship, and Aristotle classifies three different types of friendship. I was hoping that his three classifications would help settle our debate, as well as provide insight into the lovable and crazy characters of *30 Rock*. So, dear reader, what follows is a more sober, organized reflection based on my little troupe's conversations.

We began with a discussion of the episode titled "Hardball." That's the one where the NBC page Kenneth Ellen Parcell joins Tracy's entourage. Kenneth, being naive about almost everything, doesn't understand what it means to be part of Tracy's entourage. Grizz and Dot Com, experienced as they are, know the rules. Laugh at Tracy's jokes, even if they're not funny. Let Tracy win in sports and board games like Trivial Pursuit.

And definitely let Tracy win at video games. When Kenneth actually beats Tracy at the video game Halo, and Tracy witnesses Grizz destroy Kenneth at Halo, a dirty truth emerges. Tracy realizes that Grizz and Dot Com have been deceiving him the whole time about his skills as a video gamer. Tracy is actually terrible at Halo—so bad that even Kenneth beat him with almost no experience at the game. Worse than this, Tracy begins to wonder whether Grizz and Dot Com are just "yes men." Tracy fires them and retains Kenneth as the sole member of his entourage . . . with disastrous results. At the end of the episode, there is a reconciliation between Tracy and his old entourage when they rescue him from a crowd that overpowered Kenneth. The relationship is restored, but what *kind* of friends are they?

This is where Aristotle comes in handy. He says that there are three basic motivations for our friendships: pleasure, utility, and virtue. About friendships based on utility, Aristotle writes:

> Those who love each other for utility love the other not in his own right, but insofar as they gain some good for themselves from him.[1]

We've all had friendships that were based mostly on mutual usefulness. Coworkers often have this kind of relationship. We spend time with each other primarily because of what we can mutually get from the friendship. This doesn't mean that we're being totally fake or that we don't actually have positive feelings toward our coworkers. In fact, we really do *like* them and wish the best for them. But we're under no illusion that this friendship would continue if, say, we moved to another city or changed jobs. The point is that the friendship is based fundamentally on convenience and strategy. The other positive feelings, even when they're genuine, are not the glue that holds the relationship together. The glue is the practical benefits, such as being on good terms with a decision-maker in the office or being "study buddies" who help each other do well on schoolwork.

This model of friendship based on usefulness is a pretty good way of thinking of the friendship between Tracy Jordan and his entourage of Grizz and Dot Com. To say that Tracy is self-absorbed is an understatement. He interprets the quality of his relationships through a very simple filter: how they affect him. Even though Tracy is initially outraged by the way that Grizz and Dot Com have exaggerated his wit and his skills at sports and games, and even though he initially appreciates Kenneth's straightforward truthfulness, he realizes very quickly that he prefers the way his old entourage created an alternate reality that was organized around his own fantasies and desires. Kenneth can't even figure out how to turn on the television, and this makes Tracy realize that he *likes* being deceived, coddled, and served. He *likes* being the emperor with no clothes. He prefers the fantasy world where he's the center of the universe *even if* it's totally undeserved. This is the glue of usefulness that makes his friendship with Grizz and Dot Com stick. In their case, it goes both ways. Grizz and Dot Com certainly benefit from their friendship with Tracy. They get to attend swanky parties, eat and drink at exotic clubs on Tracy's dime, and meet lots of celebrities. In fact, they get paid to do this! It's unlikely that the friendship would continue if Tracy were to lose his fame and fortune. Nevertheless, there are genuine feelings of fondness. Tracy really does like Grizz and Dot Com, and they really like Tracy. Their mutual fondness, even though real, is firmly rooted in their mutual usefulness.

Not many of us are in a position such as Tracy or his entourage, where our relationships based on usefulness are so cartoonish. Nevertheless, we have these kinds of friendships, and we *need* them in various contexts. We name them differently than Aristotle does, because the language of utility is so . . . well, utilitarian. It doesn't sound classy to combine "friend" and "utility." We instead like to think of it as "networking," and we prefer calling these people "strategic contacts." A rose is a rose is a rose. We can call it whatever we want, but the principle is undeniable. We sometimes collect friends and preserve these friendships because these people are useful to us, and we really couldn't succeed without participating in this very normal social behavior.

The relationship between Tracy and Jenna Maroney, the "other" star, provides another good example of usefulness. These two are adversaries 99 percent of the time, but they become allies and (short-lived) friends in the episode "Flu Shot." With a limited supply of flu shots, the decision is made to give them only to cast members and crew considered "important." There is much grumbling, and Tracy and Jenna see this as a chance to get on the good side of the crew. Their hidden agenda is to improve their own reputations. They enter a friendly alliance with the goal of delivering chicken soup to the ailing crew, and they also decide to put on a comedy performance just for the crew to lift their spirits. The results are predictably disastrous, and the episode underscores the real motives of both Tracy and Jenna. They used each other for mutual benefit, and the prospect for mutual usefulness kept their short-lived friendship afloat.

"Flu Shot" also illustrates how transitory these kinds of relationships can be. Aristotle writes:

> And so these sorts of friendships are easily dissolved. . . .
> What is useful does not remain the same, but is different
> at different times. Hence, when the cause of their being
> friends is removed, the friendship is dissolved too.[2]

After their plan failed miserably, Tracy and Jenna were quickly back to being adversaries. While few of us are involved in relationships as mercenary as in "Flu Shot," we nevertheless recognize how quickly some of our friendships simply fade away when the mutual benefits are no longer needed or desired. It's not as if we now hate the person who no longer is a regular part of our social sphere. It's not as if we wish ill on that person. We simply say that we have "drifted apart" and "gone our separate ways," which are softer, more polite ways of expressing that we no longer benefit each other in the ways that we formerly needed or enjoyed.

Closely related to the friendship based on utility is the one based on mutual pleasure. Aristotle writes:

> The same is true of those who love for pleasure; for they like a witty person not because of his character, but because he is pleasant to them.[3]

Most of the time, friendships based on utility also have an element of mutual pleasure. There are some friendships, however, that aren't particularly useful to us, but from which we derive a certain amount of pleasure. For example, we have friends we go to parties with mostly because they make us and everyone else laugh. They're just fun to be around, and the friendship doesn't go much deeper than that.

While there's nothing wrong with friendships that are based solely on mutual usefulness or mutual pleasure, we wouldn't want to be in a place where all of our friendships were *just* like that. There has to be something deeper in some of our relationships; otherwise, we're really missing out on some of the more significant kinds of human contact. In *30 Rock*, the initial impression is that Liz Lemon and Jenna Maroney are good friends. But what are the relevant standards for counting as "good friends"? Aristotle writes:

> Now those who wish goods to their friend for their friend's own sake are friends most of all; for they have this attitude because of the friend himself, not coincidentally.[4]

Aristotle is saying that there are some people we just love *for who they are*, period. We don't love them or befriend them because of some specific benefit we get, but instead, there's just some connection of mutual love and best wishes. Some of us have been lucky enough to receive this kind of love. Others of us are still looking to experience this deeper human connection.

At first, we might think that Liz and Jenna are good friends in this sense. In the episode "Rural Juror" we're treated to a touching scene on a casting couch where Liz and Jenna are reminiscing about the old days.

> Jenna: Doesn't it seem like just yesterday we were doing the show back in Chicago dreaming about being in the movies?
>
> Liz: We've come a long way from that apartment we shared in "Little Armenia."
>
> Jenna: Oh, it was so weird there. Do you remember that neighborhood festival where they killed a goat in the street?
>
> Liz: Yeeees! But we did have really good luck that year.
>
> Jenna: Yeah. [*leans into Liz's bosom for a friendly hug; Liz pats her on the back*]

Liz and Jenna have a real history together. They used to be roommates, and they share in each other's ambitious career goals. What's noteworthy about their relationship is that it doesn't evolve that much. Here's the pattern: Liz and Jenna are on good terms when everything on the show is going smoothly. Jenna freaks out when her ambition and paranoia collide. Liz soothes Jenna so that the show can go on. This general pattern is set early in the series, in episode two of season one, "The Aftermath."

> Liz: How you doin'?
>
> Jenna: There is no way I am working with that guy [*referring to Tracy Jordan*]. Do you know that he once got arrested for walking naked through La Guardia?
>
> Liz: Yeah.

Jenna: And that he once fell asleep on Ted Danson's roof!?

Liz: Yeah. Tracy has mental health issues.

Jenna: He bit Dakota Fanning on the face.

Liz: When you hear his version, she was kinda askin' for it.

Jenna: I . . . I can't even believe you are doing this to me.

Liz: Listen. I understand that this is tough for you, but what did I tell you?

Jenna: Not to freak out.

Liz: And what else?

Jenna: Stop falling in love with gay guys.

Liz: About *this*.

Jenna: That you're looking out for me. But it doesn't seem . . .

Liz: Jenna! I'm your friend. I'm not gonna let anything happen to you, okay? Show's called *The Girlie Show*, and you are the girl. Nothing is going to change that.

Jenna: Okay.

Immediately after this conversation, the official logo of *The Girlie Show* with Jenna's photo prominently displayed is replaced by the new official logo: *TGS with Tracy Jordan*, and of course Jenna no longer appears in the image. She goes into full freak-out mode. The remainder of the episode involves Liz doing major damage control to keep Jenna on board with the show. This pattern is preserved through the seasons, and we really don't see a lot of development in their relationship.

If we apply Aristotle's criteria, we actually see that perhaps their friendship, while genuine, is mostly based on mutual usefulness. Think about it. They're both incredibly ambitious personalities in the television business, but their skill sets are in different areas of that business. They need each other for their individual success. So naturally they use each other. That was always the fundamental premise of their friendship, from back when they met as actors and since they teamed up to get *The Girlie Show* up and running.

It's really easy to confuse (a) a friendship based on mutual utility and pleasure that happens to be a long, stable relationship with (b) the deeper one that Aristotle describes as wishing good things for the other person purely for that other person's sake. These two friendships are different, and really, Liz and Jenna started more in category (a) and pretty much remain in category (a) through the first three seasons.

By contrast, it's surprising the way Liz Lemon and Jack Donaghy grow in their relationship into something like category (b). The pilot episode of *30 Rock* pits Liz versus Jack as a David-versus-Goliath adversarial relationship. Here's Jack in that famous scene dripping with a condescending attitude toward Liz:

Jack: Sure . . . I gotcha. New York, third-wave feminist, college-educated, single and pretending to be happy about it, overscheduled, undersexed, you buy any magazine that says "healthy body image" on the cover, and every two years you take up knitting for . . . a week.

Pete: That is dead on!

Liz: What, are you going to guess my weight now?

Jack: You don't want me to do that.

That's a rocky start for any kind of relationship. But at the end of the very next episode, we see Liz and Jack inside the elevator commiserating about Liz's leadership of the creative team. She's facing a public relations disaster and is losing confidence in her own ability as a boss.

Liz: I can't do this. I can't manage these people. It was a disaster.

Jack: What are you talking about? Everybody loved your little Lemon Party. Nothing brings a team together like a harrowing experience. You pulled it off.

Liz: Really?

Jack: They bonded. Good job.

Liz: Hmm . . . Okay.

We also learn in that same scene that Jack has pulled some strings to fix the public relations disaster involving Tracy and Jenna. Liz leaves the elevator and protests that Jenna will not like what Jack did, since it required objectifying her sexuality. Predictably, Jenna runs into the scene elated at the press she is receiving for her embarrassing, objectifying image, commenting only on how skinny she looks. As the elevator door closes on Jack and Liz's problem, he whispers, "You're welcome."

This creates a pattern in their relationship: professional and personal tensions alternating with creative resolutions. With each creative resolution, the two evolve in their mutual respect and fondness. It's an unsteady and often rocky evolution. For instance, when Jack invites Liz to a dinner party in "Secrets and Lies," we are treated to his choice words:

Jack: I'm going to hold a dinner party, and I would like you to come.

Liz: Wow, that's very nice. Thank you, Jack.

Jack: I just want you to be discreet, and try not to dress like a small-town lesbian.

Despite their jagged trajectories, Jack and Liz become good friends. Recall that Aristotle describes those kinds of mutually self-sacrificial behaviors as indicators that a friendship is evolving beyond mere usefulness. I can't think of a better act of self-sacrifice than the one in "Retreat to Move Forward." Jack is invited to a corporate retreat attended only by bigwigs from General Electric. He's feeling a bit self-conscious and asks Liz to accompany him for moral support by playing the role of a "good assistant." Liz agrees to do this friendly favor, but she ends up misplaying her cards. She shows too much of the truth—namely, that she and Jack have become closer friends than they are supposed to be according to the standards of these bigwigs. The straw that breaks the camel's back occurs when Liz spontaneously hugs Jack in public the way that close friends might. Jack's colleagues go ballistic over this, and folding under the peer pressure of his corporate colleagues, Jack treats poor Liz badly as a result.

Jack: While we're here, I need you to behave appropriately.

Liz: What are you talkin' about?

Jack: Well, the nicknames, the arm-punching, the familiarity, the way you were behaving at lunch . . . you can't say "adoy" to me in mixed company.

Liz: Oh . . . okay [*with great sarcasm*]. So when I helped you win that LEGO thing, when I thought we were having fun together I was actually embarrassing you? Is that right, Jack?

Jack [*looking very uncomfortable*]: Uh . . . while we're here I need you to call me "Mr. Donaghy."

Liz [*looking angry and hurt*]: I get it. You brought me here in case you needed me, but now that you have your cool Six Sigma friends I can go back to the lake with the fat kids and make bracelets.

Jack: Lemon, you know how important this is to me. I've got my speech tonight . . .

Liz: Yeah. Don't worry. I get boundaries. "Sorry Liz, my basement only has room for five sleeping bags." Or, "No, I'll come over after the prom and we'll make nachos together."

Jack: Lemon, this is a part of our problem. I give you a simple, managerial suggestion in a professional context and I get back the second half of a Judy Blume novel.

Liz: Whatever! This place is dumb!

Jack: We're going to be back at work tomorrow. Let's not make this bigger than it is.

Liz: Too late! Friendship: over!

Jack: Good lord!

When a relationship grows and evolves, there are likely to be tensions. Sometimes a relationship largely based on mutual usefulness and pleasure evolves into a deeper relationship based on mutual and self-sacrificial goodwill. Rarely is the transition totally smooth and easy, and there are also times when we risk the worst thing of all, rejection. But whether we experience the representation of this universal human drama through delightfully over-the-top shows such as *30 Rock* or in the wondrous plays of Shakespeare, we know these deeper friendships are worth the risk.

Liz and Jack experience hard times at the corporate retreat. Jack has put a bunch of unnatural restrictions on their friendship, which is about as good as killing it from Liz's perspective. As Jack turns his attention to preparing for his speech to the corporate bigwigs, he psychs himself up with a private little pep talk that he really wouldn't want anyone to hear. Jack doesn't realize that his pep talk is actually being broadcast to everyone in the ballroom, and he is mortified when he learns that people heard what he was saying to himself. Liz, despite the fact that Jack has mistreated her, resolves to sacrifice herself for him. She gets onstage pretending to be part of an improv comedy sketch where she says, "I just fooled you all with my Jack Donaghy impression where I say crazy things that he would never say. So let's maximize our fun quadrant tonight."

Predictably, she's terrible at improv, but Jack peeks into the ballroom and sees what Liz is doing for him. They lock eyes for a moment, and we see utter admiration, amazement, and thankfulness on Jack's face. It's the moment of reconciliation where their friendship sinks into their hearts at a deeper level. As a final act of total self-sacrifice, Liz rips open her shirt and begins dancing onstage in order to keep the negative attention on her and off Jack. Back at the office, Jacks says, "I can't believe you did that for me." Liz responds, "That's what friends do, Jack. Adoy [making fun of Jack's dimwittedness]."

Here Liz and Jack provide us with a marvelous example of friendship based on mutual goodwill. It's unlikely that we have such extreme and embarrassing episodes from our own lives, but we can probably recall times when we've been on the receiving end of such kindness from our closest friends. We can also remember how rewarding (even if difficult) it has been to play that role for the important people in our lives. These kinds of friendships are the ones that we identify with a full, robust life. These are the kinds we hope for when we're really honest with ourselves. And it's not hard to see why. There's just something satisfying about sharing deep values and common interests and then acting on them for each other's good. Again, consider Liz and Jack. Deeply flawed as they both are, they nevertheless desire deeper human connections. Jack has an intense but short-lived romance with

C. C. Cunningham. He later becomes involved with the nurse (played by Salma Hayek) who takes care of his mother. Liz too has her share of romance, most notably her relationship with Floyd. Throughout their romantic exploits, we see Jack and Liz growing into confidants for each other, sharing their hilariously warped insights on life, love, and family. They want the best for each other, and they often act in ways that advance the other person's best interests.

This pattern of an evolving, deepening friendship is unique to their relationship on *30 Rock*. In fact, the other relationships on the show are firmly rooted in mutual utility and pleasure—neurotically so, with fantastic results! We love *30 Rock* partly because it makes light of some of the flaws that beset all of us: avarice, pettiness, ruthless ambition, and utter selfishness. It's nice, however, to see *30 Rock* also offer a glimpse into the more ennobling virtues that give dignity to our relationships and our lives. Liz and Jack give us hope that we too can evolve into better beings, and their flaws, far from distracting us from their growth, help us identify with their growing pains.

NOTES

1. Aristotle, *Nicomachean Ethics*, 2nd ed., translated by Terence Irwin (Indianapolis, IN: Hackett Publishing Company, 1999), viii.iii.1.

2. Ibid., viii.iii.3.

3. Ibid., viii.iii.1.

4. Ibid., viii.iii.6.

A CONFUCIAN-ARISTOTELIAN CRITIQUE OF *30 ROCK'S* "SEMI-VIRTUOUS PATH"

Adam Barkman

Sometimes a joke is not just a joke. In the tradition of the Freudian slip, some say that we mean half of what we say when we're joking.[1] Of course, everyone agrees that the purpose of comedy is to make people laugh—to entertain—and most people agree that this, in itself, is a good thing. Comedy, however, isn't as morally neutral as some might think it is. Many philosophers and religious teachers throughout the ages and throughout the world have believed that comedy has a moral impact—for better or worse. Indeed, while the morality communicated in drama is often explicit and hence can be faced head-on, the morality imbedded in comedy is often subtle and, in its subtlety, can be dangerous.

Comedy needs to be analyzed for us to see just what kinds of beliefs we're being exposed to, and perhaps endorsing, through our laughter. The morality presented in *30 Rock*—the morality, to take a phrase from Jack Donaghy, of "the semi-virtuous" ("Do-Over")—provides us with this opportunity. The Confucian theory of virtue is arguably the most influential ethical theory in the East; the Aristotelian theory is its equivalent in the West. Together they should help us come to terms with *30 Rock*.

The Virtuous Path

Confucius (551–479 BCE) was a man fully devoted to the Mandate of Heaven, which declares that people can only experience peace and prosperity once Earth is in its proper relation to Heaven. Heaven was conceived as the general abode of the gods and ancestors, all of whom are unified in their love of morality. Confucius appears to have believed that the basic principles of morality are universal and binding to all beings, including the gods; hence, he said, "He who has a moral duty should not give way even to his master."[2]

The idea is that moral principles (*ren*) come down from beyond Heaven into human minds, which have the ability to process and apply these principles rightly to everyday life (*yi*). In order to be virtuous, a person must think correctly about, and act in accordance with, not only morality in general (*ren*) but also morality insofar as it applies to the particulars of life (*li*). And since correct thinking (*yi*) indicates that all of existence is an ontological hierarchy of beings, justice presupposes proportionate equality, which is to say that justice is achieved when each person is identified (*zheng ming*), and treated, according to what he or she is. For instance, fathers have particular duties to sons and sons to fathers, and though both have duties to each other, they aren't the same duties. Justice is attained in this relationship insofar as each acts properly toward the other, and each can be said to cultivate virtue when each performs his proper duties. Thus, "to master oneself and to do what is proper (*li*) is virtue (*ren*)."[3] So while fulfilling one's duty to one's parents *might* involve Jack giving his estranged father a kidney; it would *certainly* involve not waiting to call an ambulance after hitting your mother with your car.

A virtuous person has knowledge of general morality (*ren*), understands the nature and value of all the things around him (*yi*), and treats each thing accordingly (*li*). But although the goal of life is to be happy, and happiness largely comes from cultivating and appreciating Heaven-ordained virtues for their own sake, Confucius recognized that in order to be fully happy, a person also needs a refined character (*chun tzu*), meaning that a person will also value the arts of culture and civilization (*wen*), which include a basic appreciation of comedy.

Aristotle (384–322 BCE) would have agreed with Confucius on a number of points, beginning with the idea that the goal of life is to achieve happiness (*eudaimonia*). Indeed, both men thought that a person is happy when he acts according to what he is (starting with his being a rational animal), though Confucius would have emphasized that the nature of each thing comes from basic principles from Heaven or beyond, while Aristotle would have just said that the nature of each thing is inherent in it. Of course, Aristotle would have agreed with Confucius that the gods are unified in their love of morality and he did think that piety toward them is essential. Could we expect as much from Jack Donaghy?

Moreover, Aristotle would have agreed with Confucius that appreciating virtues—especially the moral virtues—for their inherent rightness and beauty and cultivating these within the soul constitutes an essential part of human happiness. The two philosophers also would have agreed that the moral virtues are tendencies or dispositions, induced by habit or constant practice, that allow us to react appropriately to the world around us. (We wouldn't be horrified, as Jenna is, at the thought that people might find out how old we are.) And though Aristotle expressed things in more rationalistic terms than Confucius, the two would have agreed that correct reason is required not only to discern universal moral principles, but also to see how such principles properly apply to particular situations. Aristotle insisted that though practical wisdom is an intellectual virtue or perfection, it's also a moral virtue. Without wisdom, after all, it's impossible to cultivate the other moral virtues.

To this end, Aristotle insisted that practical wisdom teaches that the moral virtues are found by aiming at the goodness proper to each, which is in the mean between two extremes:

> We can be afraid or be confident, or desire, or feel anger or pity, or in general feel pleasure and pain both too much and too little, and in both ways not well; but at the right times, about the right things, towards the right people, for the right end, and in the right way, is what is intermediate and best, and this is proper to virtue.[4]

"The Semi-Virtuous Path"

The first episode of *30 Rock*'s third season begins with Jack Donaghy having been kicked out of his job by his rival, Devon Banks, and Devon's mentally slow, soap-opera-loving financée, Kathy Geiss. In the same episode, Liz Lemon is looking seriously into adoption, and so a person from the adoption agency needs to come by her workplace to see whether her work environment and schedule allow her to properly take care of a baby. As things turn out, after initially resisting the urge to sleep with Kathy in order to regain his old job, Jack resigns himself to this possibility. And after initially meeting with disapproval from the adoption agent, who sustained a head injury in the process of the evaluation, Liz attempts to manipulate the situation to her benefit to get "a do-over."

"I'm going to give Kathy the full soap opera," Jack says, "while you try to trick a lady with a head injury. We might not be the best people—"

"But," Liz chimes in, "we're not the worst." After Liz fails to achieve her objective, she decides not to try to manipulate the agent further, and so calls an ambulance to bring the injured woman to the hospital. In the end, she tells Jack that she'll try to adopt through another agency, to which Jack replies, "The semi-virtuous path—you won't regret it."

Both Jack's comment about Liz not regretting walking "the semi-virtuous path" and their combined statement that the two of them aren't the best or worst people, not only sum up the moral natures of *all* the characters on *30 Rock* (including, as we shall see, Kenneth Parcell), but also subtly, but unmistakably, valorizes "the semi-virtuous path." *30 Rock* goes beyond a Hobbesian skepticism about our ability to be virtuous or moral with any consistency. Indeed, there's something to the idea that the truly virtuous person would be naive, or perhaps even ridiculous. Kenneth's "pure morality," to quote Jack, is a case in point ("Believe in the Stars"). The "normal" or "grounded" person—the person who most of us are and, according to the show's implications, should remain—is a person who isn't the best but also isn't the worst. The truth, in short, needs to be "massaged" ("Season 4").

This is a far cry from the virtue ethics of Confucius and Aristotle. For them, the more virtuous a person becomes, the more fully human he becomes. To remain "semi-virtuous" is still to remain an incomplete human being. There is nothing admirable about this, even if it does describe the condition of most people. Moreover, insofar as the semi-virtuous path is valorized, Confucius and Aristotle would have said that it's a sign of a cynical, somewhat depraved society, for society, through all its media, should be taught to admire virtue above all else. We need comedy, but even comedy, at its deepest level, shouldn't support the semi-virtuous.

"But What Can You Do When They Tell You Not To?" or, The Many Ways to Act Unjustly

According to a Confucian-Aristotelian synthesis, justice may be defined as treating or valuing each thing or person as they ought to be treated or valued. Thus, insofar as people are equals, they should be treated as equals, but insofar as they aren't, they shouldn't be. Consequently, injustice is present when (1) an equal fails to treat another equal as such; (2) a superior either fails to lead, or abuses, his subordinates; or (3) a subordinate either fails to submit to, or is overly servile toward, his superior.

The first type of injustice—when an equal fails to treat another equal as such—can be seen on the numerous occasions that Liz lies, such as when she lied about her age while dating Jamie ("Cougars"), lied about her hobbies in order to date Drew ("Generalissimo"), lied to Tracy Jordan that he won a "Pacific Rim Emmy" ("Secrets and Lies"), lied to Jack about not calling him "a moron" ("MILF Island"), lied to increase her chances of adoption ("Do-Over"), or lied to manipulate Kenneth into helping her recover her cell phone ("Larry King"). Even Liz's condescending attitude toward Jenna Maroney's past successes belongs to the same family as lying ("The Rural Juror"). So, given that Liz has a moral duty to treat people with respect, and since lying to people treats them disrespectfully, Liz may well be acting unjustly. And the unfortunate thing about this is that there isn't a clear sense that lying on many of these occasions is wrong; or if we are told it's wrong, it's always with a fallacious tu quoque, "But we've all done that!"

The second type of injustice—when a superior either fails to lead, or abuses, his subordinates—is demonstrated in "Flu Shot," where Jack argues that the most important people should be given the few remaining flu shots. Liz objects in the name of "fairness," but according to Confucius and Aristotle, Jack is right: the most important people should get the shots. It's *unjust* to treat superiors as though they weren't superiors, as it is unjust to treat subordinates as if they were equal to their superiors.[5] Liz's sense of justice isn't true justice since it diminishes the responsibilities of her leadership, and insofar as she is shown to be "noble" for such sentiments, the show perpetuates a misconception. However, even though Jack is correct in thinking that superiors should be treated differently than subordinates, the show doesn't make him out to be moral or virtuous for this belief—indeed, quite the opposite. Hence at the end of the episode, Jack is made to admit that what he did "wasn't right" and, as if to reinforce this claim, the last scene has him getting sick as a result of the side effects of the shot. Thus, while Liz is wrong in thinking all people are equals in all respects, Jack is wrong in that he doesn't care if he, even if ever so slightly (as is consistent with the semi-virtuous path), abuses his position and power.[6]

The third type of injustice—when a subordinate either fails to submit to, or is overly servile toward, his superior—can be seen in the cases of Tracy and Kenneth.

Tracy is *the* star of *TGS* and so it's proper that he has certain rights and privileges that lesser stars don't have. Nevertheless, even the biggest stars on a show still have a moral duty to submit to the reasonable orders of the show's heads. Yet time and time again, Tracy's insubordination—his injustice and indeed, vice—is apparent. He rarely memorizes his lines, is often late for work, leaves work early, and often explicitly disobeys even Jack. For instance, in "Rosemary's Baby," Jack explicitly tells Tracy not to participate in dogfighting, to which Tracy replies, "I feel sick to my stomach about dogfighting, but what can you do when they tell you not to?" In short, Tracy is a deeply flawed employee because he is, in respect to justice at least, a deeply flawed human being. And while *30 Rock* doesn't valorize this type of behavior, there are times when Tracy's antics are laughed off—meaning, of course, that his injustice isn't properly denounced.

Kenneth is a page, and justice demands that as such he submit to the reasonable requests of his superiors, which is to say nearly everyone at 30 Rock. But he often goes beyond, and thus to a negative extreme of, just submission.[7] That is, while at times he is properly submissive (just), he is often overly submissive or servile (unjust). For instance, Kenneth is called everyone's "punching bag" ("The Head and the Hair") because he agrees to carry out the most unreasonable requests, such as going to Yankee Stadium to get Tracy nachos ("Jack the Writer"). Consequently, insofar as Kenneth is servile, Aristotle, at least, would say that he is unjust, and even, because he is usually this way, vicious. Needless to say, *30 Rock* fails to denounce this since it doesn't make it clear that Kenneth is acting immorally by being servile. Indeed, if anything, we are made to feel sorry for the "well-meaning" bumpkin since we're given the false impression that Kenneth's intentions are all that matters. We thus ignore something both Aristotle and Confucius would want us to see: Kenneth has a moral duty to find the proper reach and limits of his obligations to those around him.

Jack of Trade?

Consider the virtue that Aristotle called magnificence and liberality, and that Confucius associated with *chun tzu*, or a refined character. The virtue is found in the proper attitude toward wealth (magnificence) and money (liberality), which is to say in knowing how much to spend and how much to save (magnificence), how much to give and how much to hold on to (liberality).

Although Tracy, who buys things like gold shoes, is the most obvious case of extravagant spending and the failure of proper magnificence, his approach to money is too ridiculous to be dangerous. Jack's, on the other hand, can be dangerous.

In "St. Valentine's Day," Jack reluctantly agrees to go with his girlfriend, Elisa, to church and confession, where he reveals to the priest that "capitalism is my religion." Afterward, Elisa rightly says that he has "no faith—only business." In other episodes Jack says things like "business heals all wounds" ("The Source Awards"). Moreover, when negotiating contracts for Josh and other employees, Jack's only concern is getting the best employees at the lowest wages ("Hard Ball").

The problem, of course, is that by making capitalism, business, or money the most important thing, Jack inevitably fails to be as generous as he ought to be. While Jack the capitalist makes profit his greatest concern, Confucius and Aristotle would say that money is necessary but far less important than being fair. Accordingly, while Jack wouldn't mind hiring Josh at a salary that is less than he deserves, Confucius and Aristotle would insist that Josh be paid precisely what he deserves. Liberality is concerned with balance and fairness. Capitalism and business rarely focus on these (though they could). Moreover, and more to the point, because it's not made clear that liberality (in respect to money) and fairness (in respect to wages) are important, the show leaves us with the false sense that Jack is right to aim solely at getting the best deal he can, while Josh is right to do likewise.

What Would Oprah Do?

Intimately connected to both justice and magnificence-liberality is the third and final virtue we'll discuss: piety, which has to do with proper respect toward one's parents and the gods or God. This virtue is connected with justice since for Confucius and Aristotle a subordinate should respect and obey the reasonable requests of his superiors; and it's connected to magnificence-liberality since people are expected to give their ancestors and the gods particular gifts—which, of course, cost money.

As for the first recipients of piety—parents—Jack's attitude toward his mother is the best example of the semi-pious path. On the one hand, Jack is often hostile toward his overbearing mother, not wanting her to have a phone so she won't call him, not wanting her to stay at his house when she visits, hesitating (for eight minutes!) to call 911 when he hits her with his car ("Christmas Special"), spending extra time at work so as to avoid her at home, and so on. On the other hand, Jack *does* pick up the phone when she calls, he *does* let her stay at his house, he *does* call 911 when she's hit, and he even tells his mother he loves her on at least one occasion. Jack certainly doesn't have the virtue of piety, but he doesn't just cut his mother off completely either. He is semi-pious toward his mother.

As for the second recipients of piety—the gods or God—the overall mood of the show ranges from impious to semi-pious. Three cases warrant some comment: Jack's nominal Catholicism, Kenneth's hick Protestantism, and Liz's general spiritualism.

Jack was raised a Catholic but has long since abandoned the faith in all but name. It's no surprise, then, that in "The Fighting Irish," when Tracy converts to Catholicism because of the ease of receiving forgiveness, Jack tries to uncovert him on account of the "crushing guilt" that comes with being Catholic. After Jack's appeal, Tracy gives up his Catholicism and Jack, looking heavenward, might show some sign of guilt. The impressive layers of humor about guilt aside, this episode—and others, such as when Jack delights in making a priest uncomfortable at confession ("St. Valentine's Day")—clearly has no problems with poking fun at some of the most important teachings of a major religion. And while most people probably assume such humor is acceptable (hence the counter-outrage over the Muslims' reaction to the *Jyllands-Posten* Muhammad cartoon controversy), it isn't clear that such humor *is* morally acceptable. Indeed, Confucius and Aristotle both thought that to take religion and devotion to the gods too lightly is blasphemous and a sign of impiety—that is, a failure to render due respect to the gods.

When we look at Kenneth's attitude toward religion, the general climate of impiety slightly improves, but not much. On the one hand, Kenneth appears pious since he tries to do what he believes—rightly or wrongly—God would have him do, such as not drinking hot liquids because "it's the Devil's temperature" ("Episode 210"), not lying ("MILF Island"), putting "duty before self" ("Cooter"), and even willing to give his life so that others can live ("Believe in the Stars"). On the other hand, his apparent piety is constantly undermined, since it's shown to be grounded not in practical wisdom but rather in naivety and ignorance. Hence, we're told with a slightly smug secular humanistic "nudge, nudge" that he went to "Kentucky Mountain Bible College" ("The C Word") and that his favorite subject in high school was science, "especially the Old Testament" ("Kidney Now!"). Indeed, when Kenneth says things like "When has religion ever caused any trouble?" ("Christmas Special"), we're immediately supposed to see that Kenneth is naive and hence his piety, in turn, is a bit foolish. Thus, even though Jack says that in moral matters Kenneth is his "hero" ("Believe in the Stars"), the show seems to valorize Jack's impiety at least as much as Kenneth's foolish and, hence false, piety.

Even more semi-pious than Jack or Kenneth is Liz. In "The Source Awards," Tracy asks her about her religion, to which she replies, "I pretty well do whatever Oprah tells me," (an echo of sentiments in "Hard Ball," where it's asked in the manner of Evangelical Christianity, "What would Oprah do?"). While this is an obvious pun about the spiritual milieu of many middle-aged American women, this attitude successfully reflects the semi-pious state that is implicitly championed by the show. The attitude is one of general spirituality (hence Jack's cynicism is bad), yet this spirituality shouldn't have too much content (hence Kenneth's Bible-thumping is rejected). Consequently, whereas Confucius and Aristotle would have said that the more often and sincerely a person honors the gods, the more likely it is that he or she is pious and hence admirable, Liz thinks it's "weird" that Floyd goes to church on a Tuesday ("Fireworks"), and Elisa is portrayed as ridiculous for saying to Jack, "Don't tell me you're one of the those convenient Catholics who only goes to church every Sunday" ("St. Valentine's Day").

"Well, It Got Big Laughs"

Even comedy must approach virtue with respect. So despite being the funniest show on TV, *30 Rock* may also be considered a bit of a failure in that it often implicitly valorizes the semi-virtuous—instead of the virtuous—path. Indeed, while I didn't have time to examine any of the virtues save for those associated with justice, I couldn't find any of the show's characters to have any of the Confucian-Aristotelian virtues. Yes, Kenneth appears pious, but he is clearly a fool and hence can't be considered genuinely pious because all virtues require wisdom. Yes, Pete and Tracy don't cheat on their wives, but they both seriously consider it and hence can't be called temperate; and so on.

I realize that in this chapter, I may be playing Liz to the reader's Jack—writing "an appeal to a return to common sense and decency" only to have the reader say as Jack does, "Well, it got big laughs" ("Fireworks"). Nevertheless, Confucius, Aristotle, and indeed many of the world's philosophers and religious leaders would challenge fans of even the most enjoyable, seemingly harmless shows, to approach them with an eye toward the larger issue: how morality and virtue are represented. Not everything is a laughing matter.

NOTES

1. Freud defends this claim in his *Jokes and their Relation to the Unconscious*, edited by James Strachey (New York: W.W. Norton and Co., 1990).

2. Confucius, *Analects*, translated by Edward Slingerland (Indianapolis: Hackett, 2003), 15.35.

3. Ibid., 12.1.

4. Aristotle, *Nicomachean Ethics*, translated by Hugh Fredrick (Toronto: Penguin, 2004), 1106B18-24.

5. Compare this to "Retreat to Move Forward," where one of the Six Sigmas reminds Jack that it's inappropriate for a boss to be *too* familiar with his subordinates; or with "The Natural Order," where Tracy attempts to show Liz the error of thinking that everyone should be treated equally.

6. Another example of Jack's abuse of his subordinates is when he uses Kenneth as gay-bait for Devon, thus humiliating him "for television" ("Fireworks").

7. Of course, Kenneth isn't the only servile character on *30 Rock*: Grizz and Dot Com are Tracy's yes men; and Liz, despite her spunk, wins the "GE Followship Award" ("Rosemary's Baby") for slavishly toeing the company line by using "pos-mens" ("positive mentions," a form of product placement) to promote the mother company's other products ("Jack-Tor").

PART TWO

THE GIRLIE SHOW: GENDER, RACE, AND SEXUAL ORIENTATION AT *30 ROCK*

RACE AT THE ROCK: RACE CARDS, WHITE MYTHS, AND POSTRACIAL AMERICA

J. Jeremy Wisnewski

Imagine that your TV goes on the fritz and won't show any images. *30 Rock* is funny enough, of course, so you'll still tune in, even though you won't see what hats Frank wears, or Kenneth's near-magical goofiness.

Even if you'd never seen the show before, you'd know Tracy Jordan was black. You wouldn't know this because of stereotypical speech patterns—things that anyone can choose to use or not to use (Bryant Gumbel and Eminem, anyone?). You'd know Tracy Jordan was black because he'd *tell you so*. He's bringing "the black back to NBC," after all ("Pilot"). If you talked to Tracy long enough, there's also a good chance he'd call you a racist. Tracy lets the accusation of racism fly freely.

> Tracy Jordan: You know how pissed off I was when *U.S. Weekly* said that I was on crack? That's racist! I'm not on crack—I'm straight-up mentally ill! ["Pilot"]

Liz Lemon: Tracy, do you think I'm racist?

Tracy Jordan: No. I think you like to dress black men as Oprah as part of your effort to protect our dignity. ["Source Awards"]

As bizarre as some of Tracy's accusations are, he might be on to something. As hard as we try to avoid it, we may harbor racist assumptions—no matter what color we are.

Meet Mr. Black

Of course, the crew at *30 Rock* doesn't *want* to be racist. When Liz starts dating Stephen Black, for example, she goes out of her way to avoid even *seeming* racist. When Stephen drops by Liz's office to confirm their date, Jack is impressed.

Jack: Well, well, well, Lemon . . . Stephen's a good man. He's on partner-track at Dewey, and he's a Black.

Liz: A black? That is *offensive*.

Jack: No, no. That's his last name. Stephen Black. Good family.

Liz: Oh yeah, of course.

Jack: A remarkable people, the Blacks. Musical, very athletic, not very good swimmers—again, I'm talking about the family. Black is African-American, though.

Liz: Well, I don't care about that.

Jack: Well, I know that is the kind of thing we tell ourselves. But trust me. When I was dating Condoleezza there were genuine cultural tensions. I mean, we would go to the movies and she would yell at the screen . . .

Liz: I don't even notice those kinds of things. When I leave work, I'm just riding on a subway car with scary, teenage *people*. ["The Source Awards"]

Jack's seeming racism, describing the Blacks and Condo-leezza "yelling at the screen" when he took her to the movies, is amusing. Jack also manages to remind us that we can't always control our responses to others. As he hints, the reality of racism is independent of our intentions. Racism can pop up even when we're expressly trying to *avoid* it. This might be what's driving Stephen Black's worry about Liz's ideas of race. Despite Liz's assurance that she's not racist, racism can sometimes sneak into our thinking despite our best efforts to prevent it.

Liz: You're obviously a really nice guy. But I just don't think we're a very good match.

Stephen: Yeah, I know. I get it. [*pauses*] It's because I'm black.

Liz: What!?

Stephen: I said, "I get it." [*raising voice*] You don't like me because I'm black!

[*Everyone at restaurant gasps.*]

Liz: You think I'm a racist? [*whispering to herself*] That is just nasty, negative . . .

Stephen: What did you just call me under your breath?

Liz: Nothing! I'm not racist! I love black men. I love you. This is fantastic! Let's get dessert. Yeah. Death by chocolate . . . no, no . . . not that kind of chocolate!

Of course, Mr. Black's worries seem to stem from being genuinely oblivious to his incompatibility with Liz. He blogs about Star Wars (the Strategic Defense Initiative, not the movie with "monsters"). He doesn't own a TV. Liz's life is TV, and she's as liberal as they come. Stephen Black's misunderstanding of the situation is on full display when Liz tries to break things off with him for the second time.

Liz: Look. I need you to understand something. I don't want to go out with you, and it has nothing to do with your race.

Steven [*laughs*]: Okay.

Liz: Steven, listen to me, okay? And please, believe what I'm saying. I truly don't like you . . . as a person. Can't one human being not like another human being? Can't we all just not get along?

Steven: Liz, I wish it could be like that. And maybe someday our children, or our children's children, will hate each other like that. But it just doesn't work that way today.

Liz: So what you're saying is that any woman who doesn't like you is a racist?

Steven: No! No, no, no, no, no, no, no. Some women are gay.

Liz [*sighs*]: Okay. How gay is this? I'm going to the Source Awards tomorrow night.

Steven [*laughing*]: Well, let me get on the black phone and call the NAACP so they can just send you your medal right now.

Liz: Okay, you know what? You're going with me as my date. And you will see that we don't get along *as people*.

Stephen: Okay. Will there be a gift bag?

Liz: Probably.

Stephen: Because you can have everything in it. I collect tote bags.

[*Liz sighs and walks away.*]

Stephen Black has probably got Liz wrong, and he probably deserves to get shot in the butt (and to have his pants ruined) when he acts like an ass at the Source Awards. But he isn't wrong to look out for racism even in the most liberal of people.

The Accidental Racist

When Liz wants to compliment Tracy's wife, Angie, on her new diamond ring, she puts her compliment in street slang, saying, "Bling, bling, that is ghetto fabulous." Angie replies indignantly that "this belonged to Brooke Astor!" ("The Collection"). The retort reveals some of Liz's assumptions—assumptions about how African Americans talk, how they want to be addressed, and what they take pride in. Liz, good liberal that she is, quickly sees her mistake. She doesn't want to seem racist, and she tries to do everything in her power to prevent it. She's ashamed of her remark, and immediately regrets it.

But this isn't the only instance when Liz (or other members of the cast and crew) step into inadvertent racism. When Tracy won't read his cue cards, for example, Jenna begins to think Tracy can't read. While Liz at first calls the suggestion offensive, she quickly buys into it.

Liz: Tra . . . can you read?

Tracy: Can I *read*?

Liz: Please don't get angry. It's not your fault. It's the system. Did you ever see *Hoop Dreams*? It's like that.

Tracy: So you're asking me if I'm illiterate!?

Liz: You don't even have to answer me if you don't want to. Just know that if you need a tutor, we will get you a tutor. If you need to be in fewer sketches until you get more confident, we'll accommodate you. Whatever you need.

Tracy: So I could, like, leave work early if I need a tutor?

Liz: Absolutely. We'll work around your schedule.

Tracy: I can't read Liz Lemon! My shameful secret is out . . . now you know why I'm always running into the ladies' bathroom. [*walks into hallway, screaming*] I can't read! I sign my name with an X! I once tried to make mashed potatoes with laundry detergent! I think I voted for Nader! [*screaming louder*] Nader! ["Jack-Tor"]

Of course, the ruse doesn't last long. Liz sees Tracy reading the paper in the elevator only seconds later. Of course, there's some evidence that Tracy can't read: he won't read cue cards, he fills out the crossword with smiley-faces, and he won't read things when asked to. Is it wrong to think he's illiterate? Well, in a word, *yes*—if the thought behind this has to do with Tracy's race. The danger, as we've noted, is that we don't know all of our thoughts about race. Some of them are just unconscious reactions. In this respect, we've got to worry even when we think Tracy's trying to get out of work.

Pete: Why would Tracy pretend to be illiterate?

Liz: To get out of coming to work!

Pete: Oh, so first you thought he was illiterate, and now you think he's lazy!? Jeez . . . you are racist.

Liz: No. Tracy took advantage of my white guilt, which is to be used only for good, like overtipping and supporting Barack Obama.

Tracy sums up the problem nicely by quoting Bill Cosby (though he calls him Bing Crosby) when Liz finally busts him. We've got to fight the "subtle racism of lowered expectations" as well as the overt racist attitudes that we find in organizations like the KKK.

So racism isn't just about what we consciously think. It's also about *how* we think, and it's about what we do. In this respect, we shouldn't be surprised to learn that even *Tracy* seems, in certain ways, to live according to racist stereotypes. He is arguably no less of a racist than Liz Lemon. To be a black superstar, he feels compelled to live out certain stereotypes. Though he loves his wife, and confesses to always being faithful to her, he *pretends* that he's a sex-addicted maniac. He pretends that he's out of control and unpredictable (remember his face tattoo?).

These are stereotypes of blacks that go back at least two hundred years: the sexual, animalistic African, exotic seducer of white women. The philosopher and social theorist Frantz Fanon (1925–1961) refers to this as the "sexual myth" surrounding black men. As Fanon puts it, "The white man is convinced that the Negro is a beast; if it is not the length of the penis, then it is the sexual potency that impresses him"—both of which, Fanon insists, are mere racist clichés that separate whites from other races.[1]

Malcolm X claimed, with some justification, that he was really sentenced to a lengthy prison sentence for sleeping with a white woman (not for burglary). The judge of the case couldn't bear the thought of the "sexualized Negro" "having" a white woman. Tracy seems to reinforce these archaic ideas about black virility and animality: he pretends to be sex-starved and out of control. He wants to demonstrate his membership in his race by playing up its stereotypes. He can be "really" black by *performing as others expect blacks to behave*—something Toofer, of course, doesn't do.

> Toofer [*complaining to Liz*]: Surely our massive conglomerate parent company could spring for a samovar of coffee.
>
> Frank: Yeah, or, like, a big coffee dispenser!
>
> Toofer [*condescendingly*]: That's what a samovar is.

Frank: Are there other black nerds, or is it just you and Urkel?

[*Toofer just stares at Frank.*]

African Americans aren't nerds, the stereotype goes. Even Toofer's *name* is a stereotype about the worth of diversity. Toofer is both black and a graduate of Harvard—he's a "two-for-one" deal: NBC gets a black guy and an Ivy League graduate by hiring just one person. This is a good deal for NBC, apparently—and the cast and crew of *TGS* use this fact as the basis for Toofer's moniker. But Frank's joke has a bite to it as well: Toofer isn't "really" black—or at least he isn't as authentically black as Tracy. The underlying assumption is that to *be black* means to behave a certain way, not just to have a certain complexion.

The stereotypes surrounding blacks in general, and African Americans in particular, are all over *30 Rock*. Liz worries about them, Jack sometimes articulates them, and Tracy both instantiates and is angered by them. But is there anything *beneath* these stereotypes? If we identify race characteristics largely by stereotypical behaviors, how should we understand race itself?

Tracy Jordan Is Not Black: Racism and Racialism

Leo Spaceman: These DNA results show that genetically you're mostly white.

Tracy: That's ridiculous. My whole persona is based on an in-depth analysis of the differences between black and white. ["Fireworks"]

When Tracy dials the phone just like a white person (according to an earlier impersonation he had done), he can only scream. But there's more to scream at than Tracy knows. As usual, Dr. Spaceman has it wrong. There is no genetic way to identify race. Tracy's subsequent obsession with his "inner whiteness" is based on some essentialist thinking about race: Tracy thinks he's biologically determined to be either a white man or a black man, and this can only lead him to confusion.

Tracy: I can't do this sketch!

Frank: What? Why?

Tracy: Because you can't have a white dude playing a criminal! That's a negative portrayal of my people!

Toofer: Tracy, you're not white . . .

Tracy: I don't know who I am anymore! There's been a black man inside of me for a long time, now there's a white guy up in here too! It's like an audience for a Bobby McFerrin concert up in here.

Tracy is an essentialist about race. He thinks race defines him entirely. This view, which has been called "racialism" by the contemporary philosopher Kwame Anthony Appiah, lurks at the core of a continued misunderstanding of the problem of race. Racialism involves the belief that

> we could divide human beings into a small number of groups, called "races," in such a way that the members of these groups shared certain fundamental, heritable, physical, moral, intellectual, and cultural characteristics with one another that they did not share with members of any other race.[2]

As Appiah goes on to argue, no such groups exist. Indeed, grouping races "for biological purposes, your classification will contain almost as much human genetic variation as there is in the whole species."[3] The most we can classify as a "race" is a group of partially reproductively isolated people. As Appiah points out, though, this means that "no large social group in America is a race."[4]

Appiah's view is not a minority one (the pun's there, do with it what you will). There's actually a great deal of agreement now among biologists that races are not biologically real. The problem is that we seem to be stuck thinking that they *are* real. This, as we've seen, can lead people to adopt, or even to be forced into, particular kinds of identities.

> Once the racial label is applied to people, ideas about what it refers to, ideas that may be much less consensual than the application of the label, come to have their social effects. But they have not only social effects but psychological ones as well; and they shape the ways people conceive of themselves and their projects.[5]

Behind our thinking about race, then, is a kind of *racialism*—the view that race is essential to who one is and what one does. We can see this, for example, in our reactions to Tracy Jordan deciding to play the part of Thomas Jefferson in the epic biopic *Jefferson*.

Why is it so difficult for us to imagine Tracy Jordan playing Thomas Jefferson? Is it that we recognize his failings as an actor? Is it that we think of old T.J. as a noble aristocrat and Tracy as a buffoon? Or is it—let's be honest—that we think T.J. is really, deeply, essentially, *white*? If Tracy Jordan can't play T.J. because of his race, we must think that race is somehow crucial to who one is. Someone might also say that a woman could not play T.J. because old T.J. was essentially a man, and to present him as a female would be to ignore this. Tracy actually accepts this view. He feels compelled to paint himself white, as though whiteness were some innate quality that Jefferson possessed.

Tracy's struggles with his inner whiteness come to an end when he dreams of a meeting with Thomas Jefferson: "Dream Jefferson told me some amazing stuff. It's not about who you were. It's about who you are *right now*" ("Fireworks"). But this doesn't end the debate about racism. After all, there's still a lot of discrimination based on the *false idea* that races are essential to who one is. So even being a certain way *right now* doesn't alleviate the inequality that has been sustained in our social institutions. It likewise doesn't make racial prejudice go away.

Jenna Is Black

After Jenna decides to sue Tracy for her share of the profits from Tracy's wildly successful porno video game, the two stars of *TGS* find themselves in mediation. Here is how they characterize the dispute:

> Jenna: Tracy thinks he can treat me unfairly because I'm a woman.
>
> Tracy: What? Please. We are here because white folks think they can do whatever they want to do to black folks. It's like when Adrien Brody kissed Halle Berry at the Oscars. White people stole jazz, rock 'n' roll, Will Smith, and heart disease. Now they think they can take my hard-earned money.
>
> Jeffrey (the mediator): Okay. Well, if we look at how voice actors are normally compensated . . . [*places information on the table in front of Tracy and Jenna*]
>
> Jenna: Liz says these days in America it's harder to be a woman than a black man!
>
> Tracy: Liz Lemon? That chick is dumb.
>
> Jeffrey [*trying to intervene*]: Okay . . .
>
> Jenna [*standing*]: Tracy, do you know that women still get paid less than men for doing the same job?
>
> Tracy [*also standing*]: Do you know that it's still illegal to be black in Arizona?

Jeffrey [*also standing, starting to shout*]: Do you have any idea how hard it is to be an overweight transgender in this country? ["Believe in the Stars"]

And so the debate about who has it worse just continues—in fact, it escalates:

Tracy: If it weren't for your people I'd still be in Africa. Gorgeous, politically stable Africa . . .

Jenna: My people? Women are the oppressed ones. And it's even harder being a beautiful woman. Everyone assumes I don't try a bit. It's discrimination.

Tracy: Whatever. You couldn't last one day in my shoes, Maroney. Right, Toof?

Toofer [*in background*]: No thank you.

Jenna: I could totally be black! You should try being a white woman!

Tracy: Okay, I will!

Grizz: No no no no no!

Dot Com: I don't like where this is heading!

Tracy: Freaky Friday, social experiment.

Jenna: Oh, it's on!

The social experiment, of course, is doomed to failure. The egos of its enactors simply get in the way.[6] In the end, it takes the mediation skills of a tween named Pam (who Liz mistook for Oprah on an airplane trip) to set things right.

Does anyone understand the complexities of race at *30 Rock*? Surprisingly, Jack Donaghy understands some of the issues at stake. While singing the praises of the white man—who makes "all the tough decisions"—Kenneth objects. Jack quickly stops him by claiming that he's *not* actually a white man at all. He's in the socioeconomic class of a Latina woman. Whiteness, Jack implies, signifies those with political and economic power. It doesn't signal some genetic configuration. In this respect, the issue between Jenna and Tracy doesn't really capture the difficulties of most African Americans or women. Many difficulties of being a minority, Jack suggests, are often more about economic and social class than they are about skin color or sex.

Of course, Jack doesn't always recognize this—and he doesn't always understand how to deal with social and economic disparity. When he tries to take over Tracy's community service coaching of a Knuckle Beach baseball team, Jack gets it all wrong. He thinks a few inspirational words and a new uniform will conquer generations of inequality ("Cougars"). As we see from the disaster that ensues, it'll take more than some corporate sponsorship to end the inequality that pervades race relations.

Tracy makes his share of mistakes too. While it's true that race bubbles up into our decisions in ways we're unaware of, it's still possible to see racial issues where there aren't any.

Kenneth: You can't eat candy if you have diabetes.

Tracy: There's no link between diabetes and diet. That's a white myth, Ken, like Larry Bird or Colorado. ["Retreat to Move Forward"]

Likewise, it's possible to see racial issues in ways that make matters worse rather than better.

Tracy: Affirmative action was designed to keep women and minorities in competition with each other to distract us while white dudes inject AIDS into our chicken nuggets. ["Pilot"]

Whatever the problems associated with affirmative action programs, these programs hardly have anything to do with chicken nuggets, even in the worst possible scenario.

Tracy Plays the Race Card

The fact that race is socially real but biologically spurious makes issues of racial equality all the more difficult. On the one hand, we want to promote racial equality. On the other, we want to deny that there is anything that really counts as a race. The situation seems to require something like double-talk: we want to have race and do away with it too. Tracy wants to be who he is *right now*, but he also can't help but think of himself as part of a long history of racism—a history that has consequences in the present.

> Tracy: I took my son to his cello recital this morning at what turned out to be midnight yesterday. White oppressors, answer my question *really*. What time is it?
>
> Pete: 2:45 P.M.
>
> Tracy: You're a bunch of racists.
>
> Liz: What? How did we jump to that already?
>
> Tracy: You treat me like a child! No, worse than that. You treat me like one of those little pageant girls with the clip-on teeth.
>
> Liz: No, no. Oprah says that you teach people how to treat you. And this is what you've taught us, because you're always late and you take no responsibility for your actions.
>
> Tracy: Irregardless! You know what? [*pulls card from his jacket that says "Race Card"*] Race card!
>
> [*Tracy hands his Race Card to Liz.*]
>
> Pete: No, no! Don't accept it!
>
> [*Liz takes card, Pete sighs, and Tracy puts his hands up and walks away.*] ["The Natural Order"]

If races aren't real, is Tracy wrong to appeal to race? Not at all. The idea of race is *socially* real, and it has very real consequences. If the ultimate goal is equality, we don't need any biological notion of race to strive for it. Whatever one's social group happens to be, and however one self-identifies or is identified by others, the goal is the same: that we have equal treatment of those who have historically been treated in ways that fall far short of this. But what does equal treatment require? Both Tracy and Liz have some ideas about this.

Tracy: This is postracial America. And I demand to be treated like everyone else.

Liz: You want to be treated like everybody else? Fantastic. Then tomorrow, I'm sending a regular town car for you rather than one of those duck tour boats.

Tracy: Fine.

Liz: And, you're no longer allowed to point at women in the cafeteria and yell, "I wanna get that pregnant!"

Tracy: Fine. I'll bring my lunch from home.

Liz: And be here tomorrow at 10 AM and know your lines.

Tracy: You don't think I can do that?

Liz: We'll find out tomorrow at 10 AM.

Tracy: And I'll have the last laugh! [*begins laughing maniacally*]

Grizz and Dot Com, always paragons of wisdom, point out that Liz has made a huge mistake. She's set herself up for more of Tracy's shenanigans (to use some Celtic slang). To everyone's surprise, Tracy comes in the next day on time, lines memorized, and the picture of professionalism. After a great rehearsal, Liz approaches Tracy to apologize. Tracy stops her.

Tracy: I want to publically thank you, Liz Lemon, for you have shown me that in today's world, everyone should be treated exactly the same. *No one* should get preferential treatment.

Liz: I agree. Exactly.

Tracy: Not black comedy superstars, not Hispanics, not Indians, not whatever this guy is [*points to someone whose ethnicity isn't clear*], and not women, Liz Lemon.

Liz: I'm right there with you, Tracy.

Tracy: Good. I feel parched from being so professional. Could I trouble you for some water?

Liz: Yeah, of course. [*Liz goes to water, finds it empty.*] Brian, would you help me out with this?

Tracy: No, no. Equality. Everyone should be treated the same, right Liz Lemon? You should change it.

Liz: Right. Okay. I know how to do this.

[*Liz struggles to change the water on the dispenser, water going everywhere.*]

Tracy: No one help her!

[*Liz finally gets water onto the dispenser, but there's barely any left.*]

And this is only the beginning. Tracy goes on to tell the writers they shouldn't be holding anything back (not even their farts). Equality, Tracy surmises, involves treating people in equivalent ways—including inviting Liz to Lutz's fake bachelor party ("and a guy boss would even pay for it!"). Not to be outdone, Liz claims that equality requires Tracy to give notes on a huge stack of rewrites—something that will prevent him from attending the bachelor party. After a night of strip clubs for Liz and rewrites for Tracy, both are ready to call it quits.

Liz: Okay, which one of us is going to give up first?

Tracy: The black one! [*hands Liz the stack of rewrites he's been working on*] I can't take it anymore! I hate it!

Liz [*horrified*]: One of those strippers took off Lutz's shirt. That gland thing is no joke!

Tracy: The world is upside down!

Liz: We need to go back to the way things were, with both of us getting preferential treatment.

Tracy: Yes. We upset the natural order. You're going to strip clubs. I'm up writing all night.

But the notion of equality shouldn't be misunderstood. It *doesn't* mean treating everyone in identical ways. It means, rather, giving equal consideration to the interests of everyone involved. Absolutely equal treatment—taken to the extreme—would involve giving the same medication to everyone, even when they didn't need it. It would involve forcing everyone to watch the same movies at the same times, to eat the same foods with the same spices, to have romantic relationships with the same people in the same ways. In short, it would turn a desire to end oppression into an even *more* oppressive system in which people were forced to be *equivalent* to one another. Equality demands considering the *different* interests of people equally; it doesn't mean demanding that everyone have identical interests.

When we see that races aren't biologically real, and that thinking of them as real leads to inequality, we put ourselves in a position to give up both racism and racialism. This doesn't mean we won't use the word "racist" anymore, and it doesn't mean that inequality will just evaporate. What it *does* mean, though, is that we'll be better able to see the consequences of our assumptions about race when they bubble up—and this will give us an occasion to act to rectify whatever injustices we encounter.

When Tracy sends a gibbon to act in his place on the show, he's engaged in the kind of protest that makes us look at issues of race all over again.

> Dot Com: Tracy has asked us to read this prepared statement: "Dear racist Liz Lemon. This is how you treat me, like a white-whiskered gibbon, put on this earth to do nothing but dance around for your amusement, and reduce the insect population of Malaysia."

This may not be the best strategy for justice, but at least it's a start.

NOTES

1. Frantz Fanon, *Black Skin, White Masks* (New York: Grove Press, 1967), 170.

2. Kwame Anthony Appiah, *Color Conscious* (Princeton: Princeton University Press, 1996), 54.

3. Ibid., 69.

4. Ibid., 73.

5. Ibid., 78.

6. For a real social experiment along these lines, see John Howard Griffin's *Black Like Me* (New York: Signet Publishing, 1960). Griffin posed as a black man and made his way through the deep South in the 1950s. The results are fascinating.

GETTING GAY: HOW *30 ROCK* HELPS US UNDERSTAND SEXUALITY

J. Jeremy Wisnewski

The ancient Greeks did not have the same views of sexuality that we do. In Athens, for example, men had sex with younger men on a regular basis. There was nothing improper in these relationships, the Athenians thought. They viewed the man-boy relationship as one of mentoring. But while sex between older and younger males was acceptable, sex between two older males was frowned upon. Thus, what we call "homosexuality" wasn't accepted in the Greek world any more than it's accepted in ours. Pederasty, on the other hand, *was* widely accepted.

There's a surprising connection between ancient Athens and *30 Rock*—and it isn't in the way Frank goes gay for the coffee boy. Both ancient Athenian society and *30 Rock* reveal something to us about the way we think about sexual orientation. A look at either can, perhaps surprisingly, reveal certain things to us about our own assumptions. Exploring these assumptions can help us understand sexual orientation—can help us get what we call "gay."

Can Devon Banks and Liz Lemon Choose Their Sexual Orientation?

One of the central debates surrounding sexual orientation concerns whether one can *choose* one's sexual orientation. Part of this debate stems from a failure to specify what's meant by "sexual orientation." Some people think a person is homosexual only if he or she engages in homosexual acts; others maintain that being a homosexual only involves having certain desires (and it doesn't matter if you act on those desires). If being gay requires acting on one's homosexual desires, it's easy to say it's a matter of choice. One can choose to engage in same-sex sex or not.

The same thing doesn't seem to apply to our desires, though. No matter how hard we try, our desires seem beyond our control. Liz makes exactly this point after Jack sets her up on a blind date with a lesbian named Gretchen Thomas. Pete even recommends that Liz turn into a lesbian so that she can be with Gretchen—someone who's a much better catch than most of the men Liz has dated. Despite the fact that she enjoys Gretchen's company, she tells Pete, she can't simply "flip a switch" to make herself suddenly want to have sex with women. Sexuality just doesn't work that way ("Blind Date").

If you have your doubts about whether desires are chosen, try this thought experiment: choose to find Frank sexually appealing. If you *already* find Frank sexually appealing (Pete's right when he points out that we'd all be lucky to have Frank— he's such a sweet and caring man), choose to find someone else attractive. If the experiment strikes you as easy, choose to find an elephant sexually appealing, or the gibbon that replaces Tracy in *TGS* rehearsals one week.

Of course, it's easy to simply say, "I find that gibbon attractive!" But it's quite another thing to actually *desire* the gibbon sexually. If our desires are a product of choice, though, it should be possible to simply turn desire on and off with a flick of a cognitive switch. So if you really think desires are chosen, you should be craving sex with the gibbon right about now. I'll guess that you're not. (If you are, you've got better things to do than read this chapter.) This should be enough to convince you that our desires aren't simply chosen. We find ourselves already desiring certain things, and we choose whether or not to act on those desires. In this respect, Jack's nemesis Devon Banks greatly misunderstands his own sexual desires.

Jack: Banks, what are you doing in town? Are you drawn to the phallic nature of our skyline?

Devon Banks [*laughs*]: Very funny, Jack. How gay is this? I'm here visiting my fiancée.

Jack [*surprised*]: What?

Banks: Kathy, this is Jack Donaghy.

Jack: Banks, have you lost your mind?

Banks: Oh, did I forget to mention that Kathy is Kathy Geiss? As in, Don Geiss's daughter? Do you believe that Don thought she'd never get married?

Jack: You can't, you're gay.

Banks: No, not anymore, friend. Are you familiar with the Church of Practicology?

Jack: You mean the cult that was invented by Stan Lee?

Banks: No. I mean the religion founded by the alien king living inside Stan Lee. See, it's my faith in practicology that has led me to uncover my true, straight self.

[Cut to Banks, sensors on head, hands on a large blue crystal, sitting at a table with several others.]

Banks [*nervously*]: It's definitely working. I can totally feel the gay draining right out of me! By the eye of Zolnak, right, guys? ["Jack Gets in the Game"]

But we all know this just doesn't work for Banks. Later, when he and Jack are at Don Geiss's party, Jack introduces Devon to a young wrestler. To Devon's delight, Jack gets the wrestler to try to pin him: "You're so strong! You're having your way with me! Your back is like a barrel of snakes! I think I love you . . . we're just joking!!" ("Jack Gets in the Game"). When Banks is later tackled again by the wrestler, he joyfully gives in, crying out, "Oh God! Just like the Greeks!" His choices don't seem to have much effect on what he desires.

What We Can Learn from Devon

Devon Banks's remarks remind us of two very interesting features of sexual orientation: it doesn't seem to be chosen, and yet what counts as "normal" sexual practice in any particular time is relative to the culture and place one's in. This might seem like a pretty surprising result. After all, if desires aren't chosen, we're tempted to think of them as innate, not as specific to a particular time and place. A little thought, though, shows that these two facts about sexual orientation are actually compatible: we all have natural desires (for food, pleasure, and so on), but these desires are trained to go in certain directions rather than others. We come to like pizza rather than blood pudding, or tofu rather than cow flesh, because of the way our desires are directed by our culture.

This view, in fact, was Sigmund Freud's (1856–1939). Freud held that infants had desires and urges that were undirected: infants want to suck, for example, but they don't really care what they suck (at least not fresh out of the womb). They want to eat, but they have no concept of what sorts of things to put in their mouths to achieve nourishment. In evolutionary terms, we might even say that nature takes a scattershot approach to our adaptive traits: it's easier to have an innate desire for putting stuff into our mouths than to have an innate desire for specific foods (which would require being born with something like *knowledge* of specific foods). It's easier to have an innate urge to suck than it is to have an innate urge to suck *a breast* (which requires the capacity to identify a breast). So, Freud contended, infants are born "polymorphously perverse": they have desires that expand in every direction, unchecked by anything that constrains adult desire (shame, disgust, morality). As the infant develops, avenues of desire are closed off by environmental factors: one learns to be disgusted by certain things, to be ashamed of certain things, and so on.

In Freud's view, then, we're all born bisexual (at least!). Training makes us direct our desires in specific ways rather than others, and sexual orientation is the result. (Freud saw nothing wrong with having "abnormal" sexual orientations. While he does call homosexuality a perversion, he's quick to remind us that we're *all* perverts in his special sense, and that "perversion" is *not* "a term of reproach.")[1] Much modern research on sexual orientation backs up at least this much of Freud's view: divergent sexual orientations appear to be a natural phenomenon (surprise!). There are over two hundred mammalian species that engage in same-sex sexual relations. One explanation for this in terms of evolution is easy to uncover: it's easier to have an innate drive for *pleasure* than it is to have an innate drive for heterosexual sex (which would require a lot of knowledge about what such sex involves). The drive for pleasure, though, can go in all sorts of ways—sometimes very strange ones, particularly in big-brained beasts like ourselves. The bigger the brain, the weirder the sex can get. (What *are* Pete and Paula doing with that Pop-Tart when they fool around in Liz Lemon's bed?)

But we don't want to be too reductionist about this complex process. It would be too easy to say that one's sexual orientation comes from being raised in certain environments. It turns out that while different environments might explain the difference between the sexual practices of the Greeks and our sexual practices, it *doesn't* explain the sexual differences between gay and straight men and women in the same society. There's no magic formula, genetic or environmental, for homosexuality. There's no gay gene, and there's no evidence that being raised by one sexual orientation increases the likelihood of *becoming* that sexuality. So how does a person become gay? Aside from ruling out choice, we really don't know the details.[2]

Homophobia, Anyone?

Why does it matter if we "get gay"? Why is this even in a book about philosophy and *30 Rock?* When did philosophy become *gay?* (Ahem . . . ancient Greece, anyone?)

The straightforward answer to the above question is twofold: sexual orientation raises both metaphysical and ethical issues. Metaphysics deals with questions concerning what sorts of things reality is composed of. In this sense, we can ask questions about sex and sexuality: do these categories name *real* things? Are they real in the same way that stars and planets are real, or are they things more like money and stop signs? That is, does the category of "sexual orientation" tell us something about the world apart from human practices, or is the idea of "sexual orientation" just something that is socially constructed?

The answer to the metaphysical question may well have implications for the way sexual orientation figures into our ethical deliberation. Same-sex marriage is one of the major political issues of our day. Many people object to same-sex marriage because they view it as somehow "unnatural." But if sexual orientation (or biological sexes, for that matter) are socially constructed, this becomes a rather silly claim. After all, money is unnatural in the same way (it doesn't occur apart from human practices), but this hardly makes using money immoral.

Of course, even if sexual orientation is what philosophers call a "natural kind"—meaning something that would exist regardless of human practices—there would still be ethical questions to ask. One such question is whether or not being a member of this natural kind has any relevance to how we treat one another. As we know from simply watching the news, hate crimes against homosexuals are an ever-present phenomenon. Regardless of how we answer the metaphysical question, we'll still need to pose the ethical one: is there any reason for this kind of attitude toward homosexuals? Can it be justified? If not, what is the basis of our homophobia and heterosexism? Why do so many people automatically think that being a homosexual is somehow relevant to determining what kind of person someone is?

There's a quick argument that can be made that all forms of homophobia are deeply misguided. If homosexuality is genetic (and there's good evidence that it's not), to despise someone for their homosexuality would be like despising someone for having blue eyes. Eye color is genetically determined. Why would the possession of a gene lead us to hate so much? Is it intrinsically wrong to merely have a gene? If this gene isn't chosen (and of course no genes are!), it doesn't make sense to direct anger at someone who's genetically predisposed to homosexuality. After all, we aren't usually held responsible for things unless those things are *our fault*.

More likely, heterosexists (those who hold a prejudice against any and all homosexuals) are bothered by the *actions* of homosexuals. What's at issue is the behavior of those we call gay. Given the diversity of sexual practices histori-cally speaking, though, there's reason to be skeptical of the depths of anger we find toward the homosexual community.

Sexuality shows up in all kinds of ways in history and across cultures. Sexuality seems to be a divergent and naturally occurring phenomenon. What, exactly, is there to be angry about when we see such diversity?

Here we find the core of homophobia: our identities are threatened by those unlike us. We are insecure in who we are and who we ought to be—and perhaps we're even curious about how the other half lives. When confronted with a homosexual, this threat promotes an angry response.

But hold on. It's not like we're all busy watching people have homosexual sex. This means that the behavior in question must be inherently cultural. After Jack sets Liz up with "Thomas" (Gretchen Thomas, that is), Liz confronts Jack.

> Liz: What made you think I was gay?
>
> Jack: Your shoes.
>
> Liz: Regardless, I am straight. One hundred percent completely straight.
>
> Jack: Well, I'm sorry if I offended you.
>
> Liz: No, I'm not offended . . . ["Blind Date"]

Something as simple as the shoes you wear can lead others to categorize you as homosexual. We tend to read sexual orientation off stereotypical gender roles and stereotypical styles of dress, mannerisms, and so on. Gay men (in the West, at any rate) are often regarded as having feminine characteristics. This is probably because they're attracted to males, and we think that only *feminine* persons are attracted to males. Gender (how one behaves) here gets anchored to sex (what genitals one has), and gender becomes central to sexual orientation. Underlying this entire way of thinking is a kind of "normative heterosexuality"[3]—that is, the assumption that heterosexuality is the only right way of being attracted to other people.

As we've seen, this simply isn't true. Same-sex relations exist all over the natural world, in lots of different species. The homophobia directed at same-sex couples is directed at certain learned cultural clichés about gender—the strange idea that if you're a gay man, you're feminine. One only has to look to ancient Athens to see how wrong this assumption is. When males can't tolerate seeing other males be effeminate—when they think it's unnatural, despite the fact that gender is learned cultural behavior—homophobia is the result.

There are hints of homophobia all over *30 Rock*. We see little sparkles of homosexual companionship (if not sexual attraction) between Liz's boyfriend Floyd and Jack. After hearing a panegyric to his many managerial skills delivered by the Floydster, Jack says, "Lemon, I want to kiss your boyfriend on the mouth" ("Corporate Crush").

As Jack notes, "Men seek out the company of other men they admire and want to be like" ("Corporate Crush"). The similarities to an actual romance don't escape Lemon. "It's kinda like you two are dating" ("Corporate Crush"). But bromances aside, the homo-social sometimes does mirror the homosexual (athletes constantly pat each other on the butt, for example). And when the homo-social leans too closely toward the homosexual, some men start to worry about their sexuality. Some guys are so violently fearful they might be gay that they act out with violence to destroy whatever might be calling their sexual identity into question. (Jack's too confident for any such nonsense, though.)

Jack's mother, Colleen, exhibits an odd homophobia. When Jack has his heart attack, Colleen gives Liz a message for her son. "Tell him his mother's here, and that she loves him. But not in a queer way . . ." ("Hiatus"). Behind all homophobia is an idea that many nonhomophobes share: that sexual orientation makes you who you are. When Devon Banks and Jack are in a standoff over who will take Don Geiss's position, Banks makes a typically macho remark.

Banks: You're going down.

Jack: No, Devon. I don't do that. ["Fireworks"]

Jack's response is hilarious, but it's also telling. He reads every remark Banks makes as having sexual overtones. He thinks of Banks's sexuality as dominating and defining not only who Banks is, but also what he says. This, as we'll see, is a core confusion in the way we think about sexual orientation, and *30 Rock* can set us straight (pun intended).

Being Gay for Jamie (or, How to Rethink Sexuality)

Frank manages to call into question two things in *30 Rock*: the significance of hats, on the one hand, and the significance of sexual orientation, on the other. Given the topic of this chapter, we'll concentrate on what Frank can teach us about the latter. After meeting the coffee delivery guy (a twenty-year-old man named Jamie), Frank calls into question his own sexuality.

Frank: That guy is adorable.

[*Everyone laughs.*]

Lutz: Frank's gay!

Frank: Maybe I am gay . . . for that little peach.

Lutz: You wanna kiss him?

Frank: I do. I wanna kiss him on the mouth, and hold him.

Liz: What are you talking about?

Frank: Something just happened, Liz.

Liz: Come on. You read *Boobs* magazine.

Frank: I want Jamie.

Lutz: Yeah. You're gay.

[*Frank shrugs.*]

Lutz: He's totally gay for . . . [*pauses*] . . . Why isn't this any fun? ["Cougars"]

Frank buys Jamie a sweater—one that's slim-fitting. He offers to help Jamie try it on, and then tries to invite himself on Jamie's date with Liz. Once Jamie leaves, Liz tries to intervene.

Liz: Stop it.

Frank: I can't. I'm gay for Jamie.

Liz: No, that's not a thing. You can't be gay for just one person. Unless you're a lady, and you meet Ellen.

Frank: Well then, I've got some real thinking to do. It's scary. But also exciting.

Frank struggles with his sexuality. He finds himself with feelings for Jamie that seem to make him gay, despite the fact that he hasn't had similar feelings for any other man. His confusion culminates in a direct confrontation with the young coffee mule.

Frank: I need to know what we're doing here.

Jamie: Nothing, Frank. I'm not gay.

Frank: I'm not gay either. That's why it's perfect! We're just two straight guys who want to enjoy each other's bodies . . .

Is Frank confused? Is he in denial about his sexuality? Is it possible to want to enjoy a young man's body without being gay?

Interestingly enough, these questions bring out some of our central conceptions of the nature of homosexuality. We tend to think of it as an all-or-nothing affair (bisexuality notwithstanding). If someone wants to have romantic relations with someone of the same sex, we categorize him or her as gay. It doesn't seem to matter, from the point of view of our cultural conception of gay identity, whether one wants to do this only occasionally, or all the time.

Of course, our thinking about identity is hardly always like this. If Jack occasionally likes to go to the auction house (when he's depressed, just so you know), this doesn't mean that Jack's essentially an "auction-goer." Likewise, if Liz occasionally goes to a baseball game (with Floyd and Jack, for example), she doesn't automatically get characterized as a baseball fan. Why is sexuality supposed to be so different? Why isn't same-sex romance something one could do occasionally without being categorized as being either a homosexual or a bisexual? The answer, I'll hazard to guess, has to do with our tendency to *essentialize* sexual orientation. One's sexual proclivities, we seem to think, are the most important feature one has. We regard them as so important that no matter what *else* one does, sexual orientation is a defining characteristic of who one is at his core.

When Liz tells Frank that being gay for just Jamie "isn't a thing," she's essentializing sexual preferences. The gay dancers who later tell Frank the same thing (when he realizes he's only into one guy) are doing the same thing. There's nothing written in the stars, or the gay bible, however, that says one can't be attracted only to certain people and not to others. Why must sexual orientation revolve around genitals rather than personalities, for example? We can imagine someone being romantically inclined only to people who have a fantastic sense of humor, or who are under a certain age, or who like to wear leather. To immediately claim that sexual urges must also be confined to one sex, the other, or both, though, seems to involve arbitrarily deciding what counts as a sexual orientation. Perhaps Frank loves people who embody the characteristics Jamie has, and it just so happens that all of these people (until

Jamie) have been women. Why does liking one male who also has this set of traits automatically make Frank gay?

To be fair, we might admit that our current categories of sexual orientation cover all the possibilities. One either likes one's own sex, the opposite sex, or both. Is there anything wrong with this way of carving up sexual identity? Perhaps not. But there are lots of other ways to distinguish sexual orientations that might make no reference to the sex of one's partners. One might like petite people, for example, or overweight people, or people with long hair. We could just as easily talk about petiteties and fatties.

Our emphasis on genitals—on vaginas and penises—borders on near obsessive-compulsive behavior. We often insist on categorizing people one way or the other, rather than simply allowing people to categorize themselves (or, for that matter, allowing people to avoid all categorization). And in an age when homophobia and heterosexism lead to violence and oppression, we might have an *ethical* reason to avoid this kind of essentialist thinking about sexuality. Even though we *can* categorize people in the either/or of homo- and heterosexuality (perhaps reducing the issue to whether a person likes those of the same sex, regardless of what else they like), we've got plenty of reason to avoid doing this.

If we want categories, we might do well to think of sexual orientation as fluid rather than static. After all, there might be more than just two sexes. If we regard sexes as determined by chromosomes, for example, there are five chromosomal pairs: XX, XY (standard females and males), but also XXY, XYY, and XO. Defined chromosomally, many heterosexual men will be devastated to find out that some of the supermodels they drool over have a Y chromosome (making them men, on one essentialist view). How gay!

It isn't any better when we define sexes in terms of reproductive capacities or kinds of genitals. First of all, genitals come in all shapes and sizes. There are clitorises large enough to penetrate, and penises small enough not to. And then there are the hermaphrodites. Likewise, there are plenty of sterile men and women (traditionally understood). If one's biological sex is all about reproduction, then it looks like we'll have to have at least *three* sexes (those with a uterus that functions, those with sperm that function, and those without either). To put the issue pointedly: sex is messy, and in every sense. Once we acknowledge this, sexual orientation gets even messier. If there are only two sexes, a homosexual is rather easy to define. But what happens when we include hermaphrodites, or the XXY, XYY, and XO? Do we have to begin doing genetic tests to determine whether one likes one's own sex? If I'm an XXY female, am I gay because I love XY men? We both have the Y chromosome, after all.

Liz Lemon is right. Being gay for one guy isn't a thing—at least given how we understand sexual orientation now. But maybe it should be a thing. Maybe we shouldn't insist on someone having a particular sexual identity, and then sticking to it, particularly given the complexities of biological sex and the vast array of sexual practices in different cultures.

Go get 'im, Frank.

NOTES

1. Peter Gay, ed., *The Freud Reader* (New York: W.W. Norton and Company, 1989), 253.

2. For an excellent discussion of the scientific research into sexual orientation, as well as its attendant problems, see Edward Stein, *The Mismeasure of Desire: The Science, Theory, and Ethics of Sexual Orientation* (New York and Oxford: Oxford University Press, 1999).

3. The term is Judith Butler's. See *Gender Trouble* (New York: Routledge, 1990).

AND THE FOLLOWSHIP
AWARD GOES TO . . .
THIRD-WAVE FEMINISM?

Ashley Barkman

From women's suffrage to reproductive rights, first- and second-wave feminism resulted in legal victories for women and challenged official and unofficial inequalities and discrimination. As the least political of the three feminist waves, third-wave feminist philosophy evolved from radical gestures like the "bra-burning" of the 1960s to the more subtle "righthand ring" statement, which is less about sacrifice for a cause and more about luxuriating in financial independence.

The *30 Rock* episode "Rosemary's Baby" successfully juxtaposes second- and third-wave feminisms with Rosemary (Rose) Howard representing second-wave feminism and Liz Lemon representing the third wave (which encompasses individuals from both the X and Y generations—roughly those born in the early-to-mid 1960s to the late 1970s, and those born in the late 1970s to the early 1990s). At the beginning of the episode, Liz tells Rose that she is her heroine and that she grew up wanting to be her, but Liz's admiration wanes as she discovers Rose's uncompromisingly comfort-sacrificing, authority-subverting nature. Liz, of course, is the recipient of GE's Followship Award (given to the GE employee who best exemplifies a follower), and though she is initially offended, her tone immediately changes when she learns that it comes with a $10,000 check. Her dignity is sold for ten grand as she delightedly accepts the award, which instantly sets her up in contrast to Rose. Liz likes comfort and she maintains the status quo.

This fits with third-wave feminism, which has been criticized for its lack of a clear and cohesive agenda and its lack of political activism. Rose, in contrast, doesn't flinch at the thought of living in "Little Chechnya" or being fired. Predictably, Liz is horrified at Rose's squalid living conditions, and begs Jack for her job back. Third-wave feminism doesn't entail sacrifice and therefore appeals to Liz with its emphasis on diversity and its focus on the individual empowerment of women: to each her own. Third-wave feminists have had the privilege of growing up with the freedoms that second- (and first-) wave feminists fought for. But being born into privilege has its consequences. Without recognizing or experiencing the sacrifice of first- and second-wave feminists, third-wave feminists maintain a youthful, almost idealistic optimism about their position in society and what they are entitled to.

Although third-wave feminism has emerged as a reaction to second-wave feminism, rightly noting a flawed emphasis in its definition of femininity (misconceiving all women as upper-middle-class and white), third-wave feminist philosophy has problems of its own. It is limitlessly inclusive in its definition of feminism, from the soccer mom, to the career woman, to the stripper, to the scholar—whether you're Hillary Clinton or Paris Hilton—the feminist can create herself. This philosophy, of course, coheres well with existentialism, best represented by Jean-Paul Sartre (1905–1980), who argues that "existence precedes essence; or if you prefer, that subjectivity must be our point of departure."[1] This entails that anyone can be a feminist, and that they can do it in any manner they see fit—by running a variety show, living in squalor, watching episodes of *TGS*, or whatever. There isn't any essence to being a woman, or being a feminist: one is free to be whatever one wants to be.

Since the existentialist, nonessentialist emphasis of third-wave feminism is limitless in its definition of femininity, a false conception of happiness lures Liz Lemon to be convinced of the possibility of being more than an individual can possibly be.

Third-Wave Feminists Inveigled: "You Can Really Have It All."

The nonessentialist, inclusivist approach of third-wave feminism allows for it to converge and diverge in various forms as it embraces women from literally all walks of life. Diversity is third-wave feminism's only essence, though this, of course, is a contradiction in terms. Women feel entitled to having their cake and eating it, too. And this leads to a crucial effect of third-wave feminism: with political and cultural equality with men becoming more and more a reality for women in the West, feminists, like Liz Lemon, want to believe that they can achieve happiness by "having it all."

Of course, the desire to "have it all," properly understood, isn't a bad thing, but "properly understood" might not mean what Liz thinks it does. For Liz, it means something like enjoying a career, a family, and more—and enjoying these all at once. For an essentialist like Aristotle (384–322 BCE), on the other hand, "having it all" would mean enjoying the benefits of rational thought (Liz is a human, and to flourish as a human, Aristotle says, is to be rational). But having it all would also mean performing the tasks particular to a woman, including those associated with marriage and childrearing (Aristotle wasn't exactly a feminist).

Unbalancing Career and Family

Always brazen and ready with politically incorrect statements, Jack labels Liz:

> Sure . . . I gotcha. New York, third-wave feminist, college-educated, single and pretending to be happy about it, over-scheduled, undersexed, you buy any magazine that says "healthy body image" on the cover, and every two years you take up knitting for . . . a week. ["Pilot"]

Liz is the head writer for a successful show and oversees two hundred people. Indeed, a number of Liz's subordinates are educated men. Toofer is a Harvard grad; Frank dropped out of law school; Pete is a former high school math teacher, and archery champ. Clearly, by today's standards, Liz is a successful career woman, a feminist's dream come true.

As Jack surmises in the pilot episode, however, beneath the cloak of worldly success lies a dissatisfied woman. Liz pretends to be happy about being single, works between sixty and eighty hours a week, and doesn't have much opportunity to date. Her reading is largely restricted to magazines that address her body-image problems to boost her self-esteem. She picks up knitting every few years, which may be symbolic of the traditional woman, or the woman of leisure, something that has come into vogue for younger women in recent years. Of course, she soon quits because in truth she is neither a traditional woman nor a woman of leisure—and with little time for a personal life, she has no patience for hobbies.

By third-wave standards, Liz should be content. She is a self-defined woman, a career woman. But her pretense of happiness thinly masks her desire to find fulfillment in what has traditionally been defined as the quintessential accomplishment for women: being married and rearing children. So even as a nontraditionalist feminist, Liz is unable to escape the desire to find a husband and have kids. The problem, though, is that her career takes everything she has: "My work self is suffocating my life out of me" ("Believe in the Stars").

Liz in Search of True Love: Being Defined Outside of Work

Liz's desire for a partner is so strong that, though she is uncompromising when it comes to work, she's quite ready to settle when it comes to men. In season one, we're introduced to her boyfriend, Dennis Duffy, who is clearly beneath a woman of her caliber (and perhaps of any caliber). Besides the obvious lack of romance—she describes their sexual relationship as "Fast and only on Saturdays. It was perfect."—he is unbelievably immature, which makes her not "want to be seen with him in public" ("Jack Meets Dennis"). Despite Dennis's irredeemable qualities, Liz likes him; she doesn't need to put energy into the relationship. He's convenient and consistent—Liz knows what she's getting. He also doesn't make her feel bad about her body. Perhaps, Liz concludes, it's okay to settle for Dennis. Liz wavers on her decision to permanently end things with him until she sees him on *Dateline NBC* as an online sexual predator. Only then does her decision become crystal clear.

Liz's attitude toward men changes upon her encounter with Floyd. Her seemingly innocent crush takes a turn when she fires his girlfriend from accounting so that she can have a chance to be with him. When Liz stalks him into a church, she discovers that he's part of Alcoholics Anonymous. Not surprisingly, Liz's conscience gets the best of her and she reveals to Floyd that she followed him to the AA meeting. Floyd feels violated, having disclosed many secrets at the meeting. But he is satisfied when Liz reveals all of her embarrassing secrets in turn. A happy but short-lived relationship ensues. When the relationship becomes long-distance, workaholic Liz is unwilling to sacrifice her career for Floyd.

The relationships with Dennis and Floyd both fit with Liz's third-wave feminism. The Dennis encounter shows her willingness to passively settle to avoid making adjustments and changes in her life to impress a man. The Floyd scenario reveals that Liz can actively pursue a relationship, but it also reveals that she's unable to sacrifice her career for the chance at a more committed relationship. Signs of a doomed relationship pop up in their awkward long-distance phone conversation:

Floyd: Could we talk about something besides work?

Liz: Um . . . okay . . . What's the weather like there? ["Hiatus"]

As much as she wants to find the ideal mate, she's clearly unable to make relationships work outside of the office. It's not that she doesn't care about Floyd. Consider the effort she makes to impress him with the red dress that was too tight for her to breathe in; and think of her immediate horror the next morning when Floyd sees her in her morning garb; and recall her chasing him down at the airport to apologize for the mean things she's said. Liz is not completely passive in her attitude toward men. She tries, but on her own terms. She's willing to make small sacrifices, but never at the cost of her career. Never. Liz, in season two, discloses to C.C. that she has never compromised for a man before ("Secrets and Lies")—which is evidently true, as she even breaks up with Prince Charming's doppelganger, Dr. Drew Baird, because she doesn't want to live in his bubble of preferential treatment.

Liz is the uncompromising third-wave feminist who, without knowing it, sabotages her own chances at love. She knows that she isn't content with having a successful career at the cost of her personal life, but she's become addicted to the stress, thinking that it gives her life purpose ("Jackie Jormp-Jomp"). Her job may give her intellectual satisfaction, which is one aspect of happiness for a human being on an

Aristotelian, essentialist understanding of humans *in general*, but she's missing out on other important aspects of a fulfilled life, aspects having to do with the *particularities of womanhood*. Jack tells Liz the painful truth that she'll never get married because she's married to her job ("Rosemary's Baby"), a perversity since it's the union of two things in the most unnaturally intimate manner. Though the feminist may laud Liz for her independence, the Aristotelian essentialist would claim that being independent and empowered is not the ultimate source of happiness for a human. People are multifaceted beings—relying on intellectual stimulation alone that work may bring doesn't suffice.

Tick-Tock and Liz's Big Ben–Sized Biological Clock

One aspect of happiness for women, on the essentialist view, is having a child. In season one, we discover that man troubles aren't the only thing plaguing Liz. When she tries to dissuade Cerie from what appears to be a rash engagement, she sincerely and emphatically begins to tell her, "You're so young, Cerie. There's no big hurry to have babies. There are other things in life, like having a career"; and then her enthusiasm diminishes as she continues, "and working and having a job . . . and working" ("The Baby Show"). Liz enters the conversation convinced of the merits of having a career, the alternative of which initially seems wasteful. It's obvious that Liz thinks marriage will be an obstacle to the opportunities Cerie has before her. But in the midst of her advice, she realizes the shortcomings of her own life as a successful career woman: she has no personal life. In fact, though her aim was to impart sage advice, she ends up being affected by Cerie's view on life: "You can have a career at any time, but you only have a short period where you could be a young hot mom. If you wait too long you could be like fifty at your kid's graduation." We see how deeply these words impact Liz as they later trigger a slew of self-pitying emotions that she blubberingly relays to Jenna:

> Do you think I'd be a good mother? . . . Something's kicking in and the last few months I've just started wondering if I'm ever gonna have a baby. I'm so many steps away from being able to do it and I panic that maybe I waited too long and I mean what if my junk goes bad? What if Cerie is right?

Liz's baby obsession ensues. Later in that same episode, she unthinkingly takes the makeup artist's baby home, blaming it on "highway hypnosis." It's especially clear how much she desires to have a baby of her own when she tells Pete, her eyes wide like a child talking about Santa Claus, "Anna [the baby's mother] calls her Isabelle, but I call her Nancy" ("The Baby Show")—as if Isabelle is a doll she could possess and name.

As much as she sacrifices for her career, Liz is clearly in search of fulfillment through true love (unlike Jenna, who would have willingly married the freakishly crippled Hapsburg prince so that she would be taken care of) and a child. In "SeinfeldVision," Liz justifies her compulsive wedding dress purchase by declaring that she'll do things in her order: get the wedding dress, have a baby, die, and then meet a super-cute guy in heaven. We see her need to have children especially in her deep disappointment when she discovers that she's not pregnant. She was even prepared to have her ex-boyfriend Dennis's baby ("Succession"). And with the disappointment of a false pregnancy, she decides to adopt.

Liz, the rule-abiding Followship Award recipient, resorts to ethically questionable means to expedite the adoption process by getting Pete to set up her workplace as a baby-friendly environment, and to decorate a room as a nursery with the news of the adoption agent's upcoming evaluation. When it is clear that the evaluation is not going well, Liz encounters an ethical dilemma: Bev, the agent, is knocked out and loses her memory. At this point, Liz should have her taken to the hospital, but instead she gloats at the chance of a "do-over." In "Goodbye, My Friend," she tries to convince a pregnant teen to give up her baby for adoption, in the secret hopes that she herself can adopt the baby. Though these attempts fail, she still waits in hope for the opportunity to be an adoptive mother.

In Liz's search for happiness, she often declares that she can find a way to have it all. On the day that she involuntarily kidnaps a crew member's baby, she confidently strolls down to the elevator to take a half-day and tells Jack, "Maybe it's impossible to have it all: career, the family. But if anyone can figure out how to do it, it's me" ("The Baby Show"). Yet the moment we think she has regained focus after her emotional meltdown and "kidnapping," the episode closes with her frustrated at getting on the wrong elevator. How can she figure it all out if she isn't even looking where she's going?

In "Do-Over," Liz optimistically declares, "If my home evaluation goes well, I'll be a mother by fifty. We really can have it all." Clearly, the humor in this line is the absurdity of being a mother at fifty and considering that "having it all." Still, Liz continues to convince herself that she can have it all, the perfect balance of success at work and in the home. But recall the time when she goes to find Floyd at the airport after they've exchanged some angry words. She is stuck at airport security because of the sandwich and dipping sauce in her bag. When told by the security woman that she must leave the sandwich behind, she pathetically wolfs down the sandwich— we see her shoving the whole sandwich into her mouth with sauce smeared around her lips in real time—and then clears security. This is a great metaphor for "having it all." It's obvious that Liz couldn't have enjoyed this very special sandwich, a sandwich meant to be savored. Having it all might come with consequences; one might not be able to savor any of it.

Perhaps women, especially modern women, are in the ultimate bind. Men have rarely been called on to sacrifice because of their Big Ben–sized biological clock—but women live with a seriously difficult choice in their path to happiness. Third-wave feminists believe that a feminist could be a homemaker or a career woman, but can the feminist be both and do them well? Jack is clearly aware of the challenges a woman faces when he tells Liz, "Thank God I don't have your biological need for children. That would make success impossible" ("Do-Over").

Liz Meets the Elephant in the Room

Liz says that she can have it all, but her bubble is burst with Jack's confession to her: "I'm sorry I've lied to you. All this time I've been telling you that we can have it all. The big office, success and true love . . . [But, we can't have it all] because they require everything of you. You have to choose" ("Episode 210"). The reality is that to be really good at anything, especially the two things that often define an individual—work or family (or true love)—one or both suffer at the cost of the other. Third-wave feminists believe that the woman can define herself, but to be a successful career woman, or an excellent wife (or mother) comes at the expense of the other. Though third-wave feminists may blissfully ignore this challenge, continuing to delight in diversity, they might find themselves in Liz Lemon's predicament: spending hours at the office, but yearning for something more. Let's hope they can at least win a Followship Award.

NOTES

1. Jean Paul Sartre, *Existentialism Is a Humanism* (New Haven: Yale University Press, 2007).

PART THREE

DEALBREAKER!: CORPORATIONS, PROFESSIONS, AND POLITICS

MEDICINE'S NOT A SCIENCE: DR. LEO SPACEMAN AND THE ROLE OF THE INCOMPETENT PROFESSIONAL IN TODAY'S AMERICA

Kevin S. Decker

Although we don't use the word much anymore, "quack" is a term that aptly describes Dr. Leo Spaceman (Chris Parnell), *30 Rock*'s resident medical nutcase. Like House, M.D., he doesn't let a pesky code of ethics stand in the way of recommending "wildly experimental treatments" for his particularly tough cases. But here the resemblance between the two famous television doctors ends, for Spaceman is also clearly *incompetent*. Although Dr. Spaceman seems like every patient's worst nightmare, he's praised and recommended by famous clients, like Tracy Jordan and Jack Donaghy. How can this be?

Clearly, the *incompetent professional* plays an important role in American society, which is why he or she increasingly gets more airtime on our favorite shows. From Murray Hewitt on *Flight of the Conchords* to Michael Scott from *The Office*, those who shoulder far more responsibility than they are capable of handling fascinate us. The paradox of Dr. Spaceman's popularity despite his ineptness is partly explained by *30 Rock* fans, who agree that Parnell's character steals every scene he's in. But there's more to it than this. To explain the paradox, we'll first peer closely at the values and ideals that surround doctors as professionals in American society; why are these values important, and what social forces erode them? Second, we'll talk about medicine as a *business*, part of a wider economy in which consumer demands distort the notions of a doctor's proper skills and the ideal of "health" itself. We will have to squeeze the juiciest mind-grapes of philosophers past and present to handle both of these tasks; that is, unless the powerful bread lobby stops us first!

Free Diploma Day at the Ho Chi Minh City School of Medicine

Because humans are social creatures, we're interested in theories about what holds society together and why individuals break out from the crowd. We argue in coffeehouses and on assembly lines about how customs and manners constrain us, and how much creative freedom we need or deserve. When we debate these things, we're engaging in social philosophy. Social philosophy is closely allied to political theory, because the principles of governance studied by the latter are simply a different level of organization, and probably spring from principles of social organization.

As it has been pursued in the university setting in Europe and America in the twentieth century, social theory began to divide into two camps, each signifying a different approach to the explanation of social behavior. The *third-person perspective* (or "objectivist") camp followed in the footsteps of physics and chemistry in the attempt to isolate "social facts" that could be observed or quantified. The French sociologist Emile Durkheim (1858–1917) exemplifies this view in his analysis of suicide.[1] On the other hand, the *first-person perspective* (or "hermeneutic") camp arose in response to objectivist social thinkers, who ignored the beliefs and opinions of everyday social actors themselves. While it's impossible to literally get inside the mind of another person, we *can* use principles of interpretation, foreign to the physical sciences, in our attempt to understand why people do what they do. Here, social science can be closer to interpreting the meaning of a difficult novel (or the incomprehensible title of Jenna's long-awaited indie film based on a Kevin Grisham novel) than it is to the chemistry lab.

Let's use the hermeneutic perspective to take a snapshot of what kind of doctor Leo Spaceman sees himself as. Then, in the next section, we'll "zoom out" to see the tensions that exist in the roles medical professionals are expected to play, according to one of the leading objectivist thinkers, Talcott Parsons (1902–1979).

Ironically, there really is a Ho Chi Minh City Medicine and Pharmacy University.[2] We don't know precisely *what* degree Leo received there, but in addition to internal medicine, he advertises his specializations as meth addiction and child psychiatry ("The Baby Show").[3] We learn from his conversation with a sleep-deprived Jenna in "Funcooker" that his lab work "was in the field of sleep research, mainly because I checked the wrong box on a form once." Spaceman is clearly an old-school type of doctor. He wistfully reflects, "Boy, it's crazy to think that we used to settle questions of paternity by dunking a woman in water until she admitted she made it all up. Different time, the sixties . . ." ("Fireworks") and wonders when science will find the cure for "a woman's mouth" ("Flu Shot"). In short, Leo is a textbook case of the *paternalistic* doctor: the once-prevalent type of professional who believes that his technical expertise gives him the right to have the final say in any medical decision. This kind of paternalism was exactly what the new biomedical ethics of the late twentieth century opposed.

Dr. Spaceman's paternalism is not the least of his ethical infelicities, however. He is "very serious" about doctor-patient confidentiality, swearing Tracy, Toofer, and Frank to keep the revelation of Tracy's DNA test results among the four of them ("Fireworks"). He prefers experimental treatment regimes without a paper trail, even to the point of failing to keep tabs on Tracy's pharmaceutical cocktail, to disastrous effect ("Tracy Does Conan"). Of course, this lack of documentation allows Leo to be more generous, offering pills without a prescription to Liz and Jack ("Well, it would be rude not to take one or two"). In this respect, he greatly respects his patients' *autonomy*, or chance for self-determination, a value that has emerged as central to the treatment-decision process in medicine. Unfortunately, Spaceman also takes this too far: when Tracy asks whether his DNA test will tell him what diseases he might get or help him remember his ATM pin code, Leo memorably replies, "Absolutely. Science is whatever we want it to be."

Of course, Dr. Spaceman isn't callously disregarding certain "givens" of medical ethics like Dr. Myrick, Gene Hackman's memorable character who experimented on homeless men to solve cases of spinal paralysis in the 1996 thriller *Extreme Measures*. He's simply ignorant of them. This is surprising, because adhering to certain norms or rules in any profession has at least two main benefits. First, it allows these professionals— educators, doctors, lawyers, engineers, for example—more freedom from regulation by social or governmental agencies. In essence, by generating codes of ethics, professions agree to *self-regulate*, offering special training and licensing to their members and sanctioning those who break the rules. Second, professional ethics allow its practitioners to focus on the services that are generally agreed to be most important in their field. The ethicist Daniel Wueste explains: "In general, doing their work—attending to, representing, or looking after the interests of a patient or client, for example—professionals are allowed to put to one side considerations that would be relevant and perhaps decisive in the ethical deliberations of a nonprofessional."[4] A doctor needn't also be a social worker for a homeless patient—indeed, it may conflict with her or his professional ethical commitments to do so, despite countless episodes of *ER* to the contrary.

In medicine and other fields where services are expensive or have limited availability, or where high risk factors are dealt with through expertise (engineers building a new traffic bridge, for example), the public's desire for standards of professional conduct has led to the creation of codes of ethics. Social theories can help us to understand why this is, beginning with picking out the structure of what an "action" is. According to Talcott Parsons, for example, action (as a kind of intelligent behavior) occurs when an *actor*, or a group functioning as a whole, guided by ideals, values, or *norms*, uses one set of *means* among several alternatives to achieve its acknowledged *goals*.[5] Self-imposed codes of ethics involve discussing and revising the rules that typically guide us in situations: for example, the movement from Leo's old-school paternalism toward more patient autonomy. New norms, such as a concern for bedside manner or the requirement that patients give informed consent to proposed medical treatment, will actually reduce the sheer number of means available to the doctor for achieving a certain goal. By the same rights though, the medical professional will be shielded from the worst effects of rejected means, like lawsuits and patient alienation.

For a medical professional, adhering to an ethical code presumes a certain level of competence in the doctor, nurse, or specialist. In terms of the sketch of action just introduced, this means that the doctor generally chooses the most *efficient* means to the given end, all other things being equal. Sadly, Dr. Spaceman fails this test as well. Smoking in his examination room, he desperately searches X-ray films of a chest cavity for evidence of his car keys. He nearly phones 411 to report an emergency case requiring "diabetes repair, I guess." And then there are these exchanges from "Kidney Now!":

Milton Green: This isn't correct, Doctor. I'm not giving him a kidney, it's the other way around.

Dr. Spaceman: Oh brother. Are you sure?

Jack: If anyone is giving anyone a kidney at all. Who knows?

Dr. Spaceman: You know what, I'll just remember it's the opposite of what they say.

Green: I'd really be more comfortable if you rewrote the forms.

Dr. Spaceman: No, I'll remember. Opposite! Opposite! Opposite!

Later, that same episode:

Dr. Spaceman: I was really looking forward to putting your father's kidney in you.

Jack: The other way around, Leo.

Dr. Spaceman: That's not what these forms say.

Aside from his lack of ethical standards and competence, Dr. Spaceman surprises and amuses because of the startling contrasts he provides with the social roles of actual medical doctors.

"How Important Is Tooth Retention to You?"

Unsurprisingly, Dr. Spaceman fails the tests that medical ethics and social philosophy provide in order to judge who is a competent professional. It's easy to understand why a narrowly egotistical and brainless patient like Jenna would agree when Dr. Spacemen offers bizarre treatment options. It's less clear why reasonable people like Liz and Jack continue to use him.

Talcott Parsons may have the beginnings of an explanation, though. According to Parsons, our expectations of others in any kind of social interaction can be unpacked in terms of four *pattern variables*. Role expectations follow a pattern, and each pattern comprises five either/or possibilities:

1. openness to emotion *or* emotional neutrality;
2. orientation to self-interest *or* to the common good;
3. status achieved through effort *or* symbolic status;
4. orientation to general problems *or* to particular cases; and
5. competence that is specific *or* very broad.

According to Parsons, the decisions that we make about how to present ourselves in a social situation where role expectations aren't clear involve us in making either/or choices in these five areas, or falling back on preestablished habits. However, for the professional, many of these choices are *already made*. This means that if you want to be called a medical professional by the community of your peers in the first place, you must show that you can put distance between yourself and your patients (emotional neutrality); that you don't let the solution of medical problems become "personal" (orientation to general problems); that you are oriented in your daily work to the common good; that you recognize your status is tied to your own hard work; and that you develop specific competence—like knowing where a patient's heart is, Leo! ("Succession").

Understanding where doctors fall in the pattern variables, we're on the right track to see how doctors fit into the overall *social system*. As Parsons says:

> A social system consists in a plurality of individual actors interacting with each other in a situation which has at least a physical or environmental aspect, actors who are motivated in terms of a tendency to see the "optimization of gratification," and whose relation to

their situations, including each other, is defined and mediated in terms of a system of culturally structured and shared symbols.[6]

Whew! Put that in your meth pipe and smoke it. Actually, it's not difficult to understand Parsons's meaning if we simply rephrase his ideas in terms of the social system of *30 Rock*:

> *30 Rock*'s social system consists in people acting their roles (Liz Lemon as producer of the show, Kenneth as dependable country bumpkin, and so on) in situations that are stressful, where time is key, and where people's efforts are not very well integrated. In some way or another, every person acts out of the "optimization of gratification" or *self-interest*, and some characters such as Tracy and Jenna are pathologically self-absorbed. These people's relations are defined by the symbols they all accept, like titles ("Head Page"), power (Don Geiss), or sexuality ("Muffin Top").

That's better! Now we can isolate at least three kinds of causes for Dr. Spaceman's failure to adhere to the norms of being a responsible medical doctor: when situations out of the ordinary demand the behavior; when self-interest distorts professional responsibilities; or when the symbolic role of the doctor is no longer a match with his actual duties. Since Parsons' pattern variables are supposed to bind doctors to certain behaviors even in situations out of the ordinary, we should focus on the last two possibilities: the role of self-interest and the symbolic role of being a doctor in American culture.

"My Techniques *Guarantee* Male Orgasm"

Everyone who goes to the doctor does so in the service of self-interest; it's the doctors who have to wrestle with deeper issues of whether the treatment a patient requests is really in the patient's interest. Dr. Spaceman combines the virtues of doctor and drug dealer, and blissfully avoids making the important distinction between therapy (getting patients back up on their feet) and enhancement (offering Jenna pills "that keep people awake under any circumstances," in "Funcooker"). However, despite his incompetence and lack of ethics, I think that Leo's "everything over the counter" policy is not fundamentally a function of bad character. Instead, it is a symptom of a wider phenomenon that Karl Marx (1818–1883) calls "the fetishism of commodities."

A commodity is anything of value that can be traded for another thing of value, but *determining* the value of a thing for the parties who want to trade is the sticky part. In his economic magnum opus *Capital*, Marx considers different sorts of value, including the commonsense notion of "use-value," by which we would put a higher price on a hammer that is better made and longer lasting than on a cheaply made one. But there are also other ways of increasing the desirability of certain commodities, like "Me Want Food!" T-shirts or bottles of Snapple, and therefore justifying their higher price on the open market.

Marx thinks that some "mystification" is involved, the same sort of magical tricks that a shaman might use to instill respect for a wooden totem. He writes, "The mysterious character of the commodity-form consists therefore simply in the fact that the commodity reflects the social characteristics of men's own labor as objective characteristics of the products of labor themselves."[7] Marx means that "commodity fetishism" drives consumer interest and willingness to pay more for things because products are given a kind of supernatural aura through celebrity endorsements, clever, and in the case of *30 Rock*, very ironic marketing,[8] and the mentality of "keeping up with the Joneses." Marx goes as far as to say that modern free market economies *depend* upon this mystification to keep the cycle of wage labor and consumer spending afloat.

Imagine an economy simply trading in those things that we need for basic subsistence and comfort, what Marx calls "primitive accumulation." We would soon find, as Plato (428–348 BCE) speculates in the construction of an ideal society in the *Republic*, that certain people demand more than merely the basics: "In particular we cannot just provide them with the necessities we mentioned at first, such as houses, clothes, and shoes; no, instead we will have to get painting and embroidery going, and procure gold and ivory and all sorts of everything of that sort."[9] Like Plato, Marx believes that the move to an economy that is based on commodities with *social* significance from a simpler, use-value based economy is a natural outgrowth of our social nature. But not everything that we do *naturally* is also *right*, as a number of philosophers have proved, and as the title of Leo Spaceman's sole publication, *You're Doing It Wrong!*, implies about our sex lives.[10]

Are medical services (and even doctors) "fetishized," provoking desires that an outside observer would find puzzling or irrational, like the irrational exuberance on Teamsters' Sandwich Day? For the answer, look no farther than your own television screen and the romanticized prime-time commercials for drugs you can't live without, like Cialis, Cymbalta, and Viagra. Direct appeal to the consumer by the pharmaceutical industry is only one of a number of curious results of the conversion of American health care to a managed care system throughout the 1990s. While, on the one hand, preventive services and procedures (like cataract surgery) that would have been paid for in the pre-HMO insurance tradition are less likely to be approved for coverage, the demand for better and more exotic "high end" pharmaceuticals, lifesaving therapies, and technology has skyrocketed.[11] This has led to an absurd imbalance in resource allocation decisions between care that many need, but can't get approved, and that few need, but can afford.

A large bureaucracy, using statistics and appeals to the bottom line, stands in the way of the general populace's opportunity to decide wisely about their own care. But the social values concerning status and power that enable commodity fetishism among all of us makes the selfish actions of the few seem more acceptable. So Jack expects Liz to agree when he tells her she's one of the lucky few to get a flu shot because of her status at *TGS with Tracy Jordan*. He instructs her, "Important people get better health care. They also get better restaurant reservations, bigger seats in planes—." "A more refined class of prostitute," interrupts Dr. Spaceman. By the way, it's notable that Plato includes prostitutes among the luxuries of the *Republic*, showing that even philosophers have their minds in the gutter from time to time!

"Medicine's Not a Science!"

The point of the last section is actually threefold: first, bureaucracies in medical care and other areas of life impose a system aimed at consistency and efficiency upon people, asking less of them in making good judgments. The flip side of this is that despite all its claims to being a neutral and objective science of human health, medicine is not immune to the effects of commodity fetishism, which motivates patients to ask for treatments they don't need, and to believe that medical professionals—like the experts on "crazy surgical options" at the Bradshaw Clinic ("Jack Gets in the Game")— are capable of solving problems that have become "medicalized" by social obsessions with productivity or body image. Both social phenomena are linked, or so the political scientist Alan Wolfe suggests:

> Rather than understanding that economic self-interest is made possible only because obligations are part of a preexisting moral order, [systems in capitalism] increasingly organize the moral order by the same principles that organize the economy. The more extensively capitalism develops, the more the social world that

makes capitalism possible comes to be taken for granted rather than viewed as a gift toward which the utmost care ought to be given.[12]

What Wolfe describes as the eclipse of the social world has also been noticed by the contemporary German social theorist Jürgen Habermas. Habermas, who has written extensively and influentially about social philosophy, has been critical of approaches like that of Talcott Parsons. Instead of constructing social behavior in terms of broad analytic categories, Habermas attempts to critically examine the broad sweep of social and intellectual movements in modern times to detect certain contradictions and crises. Doing so, Habermas spots a trend that involves both the forces of bureaucracy and impersonal efficiency (which he calls "systems organizations") and the cultural practices, behaviors, and attitudes that form our shared sense of community (the "lifeworld"). According to Habermas, many of the irrational and absurd contradictions of modern life result from the "colonization" (or "rationalization") of the *lifeworld* by *systems organizations*. Our attitudes and culture are infiltrated by the bureaucracy of the system—and we can't escape this infiltration. This systematic reorganization distorts and disrupts traditional and otherwise reliable social attitudes, as we've seen, to doctors and the entire practice of medicine.

The good news is that *30 Rock* underwrites our own encounters with incompetent professionals by pointing out that the lifeworld pushes back against the system. Commodity fetishism ensures that if there is enough subtle pressure to keep providing drugs like "purples from Peru" and endorsing Tracy Jordan's Meat Machine, the professionals will make that happen. So one way of affirming the truth of Dr. Spaceman's claim that "After all, medicine's not a science!" ("Tracy Does Conan") is to say that the dark side of the medical profession is found in the emergence of a market that serves the perfectly human desire to define the ideal of health in socially fashionable ways. If correct, this is a difficult truth to swallow, but it's no worse than a visit to the doctor.

Now, how about a sucker?

NOTES

1. Emile Durkheim, *Suicide* (New York: Free Press, 1951).

2. See for yourself at http://www.yds.edu.vn/.

3. Note he doesn't claim that meth addiction *recovery* is his specialty; this becomes clear as he addresses Jenna's weight problem in "Jack Gets in the Game" by offering her a pamphlet entitled, "You Do the Meth!"

4. Daniel Wueste, *Professional Ethics and Social Responsibility* (Lanham, MD: Rowman and Littlefield, 1994), 2.

5. Taken from Talcott Parsons, "The Unit Act of Action Systems," in *Social Theory: The Classical and Multicultural Readings*, 3rd ed., edited by Charles Lemert (Boulder, CO: Westview Press, 2004).

6. Talcott Parsons, *The Social System* (New York: Free Press, 1951).

7. Karl Marx, *Capital: A Critique of Political Economy*, vol. 1 (New York: Vintage Books, 1977), 164–65.

8. In its handling of the distasteful policy of product endorsements, Fey and *30 Rock's* writers are very aware of television's potential for driving commodity fetishism. The single most cynically illuminating episode on the seemingly supernatural powers that successful marketing has? Season three's "Believe in the Stars," in which Liz believes she becomes an inner temple priestess of the cult of Oprah as the result of a drug-fueled plane encounter with a chatty teenager.

9. Plato, *The Republic*, translated by C. D. C. Reeve (Indianapolis: Hackett Publishing, 2004), 51, 373a 3-7.

10. The book title is actually a cultural meme, what might be called a "mental commodity": see http://knowyourmeme.com/memes/youre-doing-it-wrong.

11. Suzanne Gordon and Timothy McCall, "Healing in a Hurry: Hospitals in the Managed-Care Age," *The Nation*, March 1, 1999, 199–201.

12. Alan Wolfe, "Whose Keeper? Social Science and Moral Obligation," in *American Social and Political Thought: A Reader*, edited by Andreas Hess (New York: New York University Press, 2002), 431.

IS THERE A DIFFERENCE BETWEEN EAST COAST TELEVISION AND MICROWAVE OVENS?: MORAL QUESTIONS ABOUT CORPORATE MANAGEMENT

Andrew Terjesen

If you haven't spent much time working for a large multinational corporation, then the idea that someone could have the title "Vice President of East Coast Television and Microwave Oven Programming" would strike you as odd. But at GE, it's a different story. The fact that Jack Donaghy's title equates television programming with programming a microwave oven demonstrates how little the corporation seems to care about the details of what the various branches of the company do.

Does Jack Know Jack about Comedy?

Jack's cluelessness about the ins and outs of comedy become apparent when we consider his own attempts to be part of *TGS*. When Jack sits in on the writers' meetings, he reveals a lack of sense for what works in a comedy show. He finds "Fart Nuggets" (a fictional brand of cereal) hilarious. And even though he was the only one who laughed (and way too much), he insists that everyone found "Fart Nuggets" funny ("Jack the Writer"). To bring himself up to speed, he does some "research" and comes across *Dilbert*. In a classic corporate move, he then suggests that they produce *Dilbert* cartoons as sketches. This is still better than offering a story about Tom Brokaw running over someone with a motorboat and saying, "I'm not a writer, but maybe there's a skit in that." And of course, suggesting that the writers should start with catchphrases and work backward demonstrates Jack's complete lack of understanding when it comes to comedic writing.

Jack is not just in charge of *TGS*, but his other programming "innovations" seem to fall short of the mark as well. Despite what Jack thinks, digitally inserting Jerry Seinfeld into *Law and Order: Special Victims Unit* and *Heroes* is not going to entice viewers ("SeinfeldVision"). One of Jack's hit ideas is the reality show *MILF Island*, but how much talent does it take to combine *Survivor* and a confessional shower ("MILF Island")? The show simply appeals to the human desire to see a drunk MILF getting knocked into quicksand by a monkey. And of course, once *MILF Island* is successful, Jack just wants to keep milking it with sequels and a spin-off talk show based on the breakout character.

It's not surprising that someone who was appointed to manage network programming from the appliance division wouldn't have much experience with the creative side of television. It is disconcerting, however, that Jack doesn't seem overly troubled by that lack of experience. Like many managers,

Jack seems to think that the act of managing can be totally divorced from what you're managing. When Jack manages a Little League baseball team from Knuckle Beach, he's only concerned with getting them to win and has no interest in their particular circumstances. Jack says, "I don't have to understand their world in order to help them. It's like this great country of ours. We can go into any nation, impose our values and make things better. That's what Bush is doing all over the globe" ("Cougars"). After Jack's ignorance causes the team to degenerate into chaos, he realizes that he needs Tracy's know-how (and several baseball players with forged birth certificates) to get things on track again.

Who Gets Credit?: The Trivection Oven and Greenzo

In the 1980s the sociologist Robert Jackall did fieldwork inside several large corporations and published the results of his study in a book titled *Moral Mazes: The World of Corporate Managers*. A sociologist studying corporate workers as if they were some sort of tribal society in the far reaches of the world provided a new perspective on the social mores of corporate life. Not surprisingly, the fictional world of *30 Rock* displays much the same corporate culture as Jackall described in *Moral Mazes*.

To begin with, Jack's job prior to becoming VPECTMOP was head of a branch of GE that was developing microwave oven technology. Although we don't know the details, it's safe to assume that there was a group of people working on what would become Jack's greatest triumph, the Trivection oven. It also seems safe to assume that Jack doesn't know much about how microwave ovens actually work. Based on those two assumptions, it's hard to believe that Jack was responsible for the development of the Trivection oven, yet he claims to have created it. This, Jackall reports, is one common phenomenon in corporate culture: taking full credit for the successes of those under you. When dealing with his bosses, Jack will take credit for what people in his division have done. It's not like the higher-ups would actually investigate to see who did what. I doubt he even came up with the idea for *MILF Island* all by himself.

Even if Jack's bosses had been presented with a detailed account of who did what in creating the Trivection oven, they would still give the credit for success to Jack. In their minds, it was Jack's management that made it possible for the team to function. But what exactly could Jack have done? It's unlikely that he knew enough about microwave ovens to spot a technological need (to direct the team or to give them a problem to solve). In all likelihood, he just said, "Build me a good microwave oven," much as his instructions to Liz are just to write something funny.

According to Jackall, in a corporation credit always goes up, but blame always goes down. Once again, Jack exemplifies this aspect of corporate culture. When his ideas go awry, Jack is quick to place the blame for his failure somewhere else. Greenzo was Jack's idea for trying to make money off the current environmentalism trend ("Greenzo"). Everything was fine as the actor played his part as the first nonjudgmental, business-friendly environmental mascot who spouted lines like "The free market will solve global warming—if that even exists." But as soon as Greenzo went off script and started condemning the evils of big business, Jack was ready to cut him loose and distance himself from the idea, saying he "knew" they should have gone with Angie Harmon.

Greenzo was a minor mishap, though, compared to Jack's big idea of having a "Salute to Fireworks" special where fireworks would be shot all around Rockefeller Center, which looked like a terrorist attack on the GE building ("Fireworks"). After the network gets heat from the mayor, CEO Don Geiss passes the blame on to Jack and strips him of the Microwave Programming division ("Corporate Crush"). In classic corporate fashion, Jack is "punished" with the loss of a title and some vaguely defined responsibilities. However, in the corporate world, titles like Vice President of West Coast Television, Web Content, and Theme Park Talent Relations are the brass ring everyone is reaching for. In the corporate mind, a title confers responsibility, never mind that things would function pretty much the same no matter who had the title. To really understand the corporate culture, we need to get a clearer picture of the nature of corporations.

GE Has Been Brought to Life . . . and It's Not a Good Thing

The philosopher Peter French argues that corporations are persons. According to French, GE is not simply a legal entity created to earn money for the shareholders who invest in it. It is a person. The word "person" in this sense is not synonymous with "human being." Rather, a person in this sense is a bearer of rights and responsibilities. So GE is a person because it contains a decision-making process that operates independently of the people who make up GE, and thus GE itself has rights and responsibilities.

People pay a lot of attention to CEOs, but companies seem to run about the same no matter what the people at the top do or fail to do. Consider what happens when Don Geiss lapses into a coma ("Succession"). Even though Don had expressed a desire to appoint Jack the new CEO, he hadn't done anything through the official channels of the company. So Devon Banks was able to step in and put Kathy Geiss in the CEO chair. While Kathy Geiss is CEO she does absolutely nothing but sit in her office and play with her unicorns, listen to Marky Mark and the Funky Bunch, and watch soap operas. Despite this, the company continues to move along and make a profit. The fact that there is no one at the top guiding everything does not stop the corporation from acting with an intention.

A similar thing happens when Liz covers for Jack by meeting with German cable executives. She doesn't understand what she is saying, but somehow she goes through the motions that initiate an offer to sell NBC to the executives ("Episode 210"). This is not what GE wanted, and so it's a problem. Of course, Jack covers up the problem and smoothes it over when he returns, because he does not want Don Geiss to know that he abandoned his post.

The fact that we can take out the head or a central midlevel organ (VPs like Jack) and still have a functioning company suggests that the "brains" of the company must be found somewhere other than in the people who work for the company. That's French's point. Now, just because a CEO or other executive is incidental to the smooth functioning of the corporation does not mean that there is nothing that can be done to affect the company. An executive who takes decisive action can change the direction of the company—for better or worse. Think of when Devon Banks tried to sell off GE assets and planned to shut down the company for two years just to drive up the demand for light bulbs ("Do-Over"). His actions would have destroyed the company, but clearly he was acting in a manner that goes against every aspect of the normal decision-making process at GE. As long as we have business as usual at GE, things go well. CEOs and executives don't matter much as long as they don't interfere too much.

The fact that corporations can function without anyone actively giving them a direction explains another phenomenon that Jackall noted about the corporate culture. Many managers do everything in their power to avoid having to take action. Remember, credit goes up and blame goes down. So there is no real incentive to take a risk. If you do something positive, the benefits will be reaped by someone higher up. More important, if you try to do something to improve the company's profits and it fails, there is a chance the blame will find its way to you. Unless you're the CEO, there is always someone who could push the blame down to you and you might not be able to find a credible scapegoat. In a corporation, an action is often all risk, with no real reward.

And when you consider the fact that the corporation will probably do something anyway, it might seem better to ride it out. If things go well, you can steal the credit from those under you. If things go badly, you're safe because you never made a decision that could get you blamed—and it's much easier then to push the blame down to one of your underlings who did do something that can be connected to the failure. Another reason for not taking action is that a CEO might not really know what to do, because, as we saw previously, they don't actually understand how the divisions they are overseeing work. If you don't know what your actions will do, it is certainly better to do nothing if you can get away with it.

Ceding responsibility to the corporate machine only gives Frankenstein's monster (or in the case of GE, Edison's monster) more power. The more powerful and independent the corporation becomes, the more it will corrupt the members of the corporation. French worries that one way in which it is a corrupting influence is that it makes it very easy to shift the blame to the corporation. It wasn't Jack who fired Pete, it was the company that needed him to be downsized to maintain the profit margin. If GE produces a defective oven, then GE will get sued. The company will be held responsible for it, not the people who made decisions that led to that defect. The corporation creates a distance between our actions and their effects, making it easier to lose our sense of responsibility. But that is not the only danger of the corporate environment.

Is It All Just a Part of "the Game"?

The more we become detached from our actions within the corporation, the less we value what we do within the corporation.

Since we can't see what our actions produce, it's harder to take pride in a job well done. The corporation itself (the "corporate person") gets credit for everything the corporation produces. When GE manufactures a better oven, the public does not say, "Jack Donaghy makes a better oven"; instead, they say that "GE makes a better oven." Plus, of course, it isn't clear we can attribute this development to Jack alone—or to Jack much at all.

The stockholders of GE will only invest in the company as long as it generates more profit than some other company. So the corporation is motivated to create the greatest profit possible for those stockholders. But the causal disconnect in the modern corporation means that the corporate obsession with status is not about whether you've actually done something to improve the corporate bottom line, but rather about the perception that you're doing it (which is why the only real creativity in the corporate world is in the accounting department). The focus on perception leads to some interesting corporate behaviors. Jackall noticed, for example, that managers would often "shake things up" when they were given a new position. We see this when Jack first appears on *30 Rock*. He completely renovates his office, even though it was a pretty nice office before he got there. As Jack puts it, "Sometimes you have to change things that are perfectly good just to make them your own" ("Pilot").

Establishing yourself in the corporate hierarchy often involves rewarding your friends and punishing those associated with the old regime. This happens to Jack when Devon makes his power play. Jack was Don's preferred successor, and so Jack is moved down to the twelfth floor ("Sandwich Day")—a humongous blow to Jack's ego since everything in the corporate world becomes infused with significance and status. Higher numbers represent higher status, despite the fact that they also represent a greater chance that you'll be trapped if there is a fire.

The quest for status is a part of the corporate "game." The fact that it's easy to think of business as a game shows how unreal it can seem. The philosopher Alasdair MacIntyre has argued that modern businesses do not value what they do or produce as a human activity with its own internal rewards, instead they focus on external rewards. In other words, it's about winning or losing and not about how you play the game. Status and wealth are the external rewards executives crave, but they have no interest in the rewards of the activities themselves. Jack doesn't run a microwave oven division because of some inherent love of microwaves or even because of an interest in technical design. He runs it because it's a rung in the corporate ladder that he's climbing.

MacIntyre's point is that the emphasis of business (or profit-making) is the end result. Business by itself doesn't have any sense of what it means to run a business well in the absence of profit. If the business makes a profit, you're running it well. If it fails to make a profit, then you're going to be fired for doing a bad job—even if the reason it doesn't make a profit has nothing to do with your actions. In the real world, CEOs step down when the stock falls even if it's a tough market (unless, of course, they can get someone else under them to step down and take the blame instead).

Many of the businesses that corporations have a stake in do have what we'll call "internal goods." For example, *TGS* is a comedy show. Its internal good is comedy. Even if no one watched their show, the writers could take pleasure in the sketches they wrote and the actors could take pleasure in their contributions to the process of bringing those sketches to life. The production crew could feel good about a well-edited and well-designed show. The fact that the viewing numbers were low wouldn't take away from the fact that the crew made something funny. At least, it shouldn't. Unfortunately, the corporate mentality can spread like a virus and pervert our attitudes. Instead of producing things that are genuinely funny, we start creating sketches that appeal to the lowest common denominator.

The Corporate Mentality and *TGS*

Since corporations regard profit-making as the only good worth pursuing, they discount the internal goods of all of their businesses. Everything becomes a way to make money. With products this is pretty straightforward: find out what people want to buy through "market research" and then create that product. By Jack's own admission, this is what he did with the Trivection oven ("Pilot"). He found out what people who purchase ovens want in their ovens (or their popcorn makers) and told the design team to come up with it. Once again, Jack can take credit for paying attention to the results of market research and play down the actual activities of solving the design problems.

Manufactured products are easy for corporate executives to wrap their heads around. Artistic endeavors, like comedy, are more befuddling. Sure, executives understand the idea that television programs can sell ad time and that they will be paid more for ad time during shows that have larger audiences. And market research will tell them which shows will get large audiences. Such research leads Jack to push Tracy Jordan onto *TGS* (as well as deemphasize its original name of *The Girlie Show*) in order to reach valuable marketing demographics that the show had not been serving. This is all well and good, a corporate suit might wonder, but what about all that airtime that is between the commercials? How is that making us money?

When it comes to the corporate mentality, one response might be to use the television programming to serve other parts of the corporate interest. For example, Greenzo can advocate for free market policies and oppose environmental legislation, which would enable GE companies to produce their products without the added cost of making them safe for the environment. The content on shows like *TGS* should be something you can sell to people on iTunes or DVD, or it should be something that can be used to sell other products. Thus, in classic corporate fashion, Jack instructs all NBC shows to engage in "synergy" or "product integration" by making "pos-mens" (positive mentions) of GE products on their shows ("Jack-Tor"). In this way, these television programs will be more successfully "monetized" and increase the "upward revenue stream dynamics." When the writing staff balks at this suggestion, Jack turns to his assistant Jonathan and says, "Oh, I'm sorry. That's right. They're artists like James Joyce or Strindberg. Get real, kids. You write skits mocking our presidents to fill time between car commercials." Jack's sarcasm may be partially warranted. *TGS* is not going to make an artistic contribution to comedy equivalent to Shakespeare or that Aristophanes guy. Still, though, it's not as if there's nothing more to what they do than take up air time.

Still, Jack can't shake the corporate mentality. He treats the show's writers as his go-to people for speeches and ideas for pitching products (Funcooker, anyone?). And he can't seem to focus on anything other than selling things (or negotiating with people over money). When he comes to the writing staff with a crisis surrounding the miniature microwave he's been working on for three years, it's to get them to come up with a name before it hits stores in just two days ("The Funcooker"). According to Jack, most of his time on the product "has been spent focused on coming up with a hip, edgy name for that product. Something that will appeal to the marketing holy trinity: college students, the morbidly obese, and homosexuals." (Apparently, the name they had originally come up with, "Bitenuker," is deeply offensive to those who speak French or Dutch, as we can see by the reaction of Ms. Laroche Vanderhoot in the writer's room.) The fact that Jack thinks the only time spent on the project that really matters is the time spent coming up with a name shows how much of the activity of microwave design is being disregarded. Other activities don't serve the only good that matters to the corporate mind—the external reward of profit created when the holy trinity buys the product. It doesn't matter all that much if the product satisfies them or works.

We also see in this instance how the focus on profit (and selling things to make a profit) can lead someone to make no distinctions between different activities within the company. Since profit is all that matters, NBC television shows are viewed as just another form of making money and selling things, interchangeable with any other division of the company. And anyone who works for them can be moved around without concern for "what they do." Thus, when Jack enlists the writers' help on the "Bitenuker," he proclaims that they're all now a part of the microwave division. And in the corporate mind, it's just that easy. Jack sees no problem with putting an entire staff on that little problem and leaving Liz to write the entire show. As Jack says, "How hard can it be?" and then rattles off a cookie-cutter overview of one week's show (complete with a killer impression of Robert De Niro as an auctioneer).

From the perspective of those who run a multinational company, there's no difference between microwave ovens and a late-night comedy sketch show: both are ways of making money. This mentality is hard to avoid for people who didn't build up the business but rather bought it from someone else. Moreover, since the corporate structure has a life of its own, there's not much that managers can do to actually affect the workings of their division (in fact it's often best if they do nothing and let their employees sort of manage themselves). But if there's nothing that managers actually do (other than be a lightning rod for praise and blame and create an illusion of control to investors), then one can assign management responsibilities without much concern for whether the person they are given to has the right "qualifications." Being the VP of East Coast Television can be combined with Microwave Oven Programming, or Theme Park Talent Relations, without a second thought. It doesn't really matter who manages what, as long as it's managed.

Too Big to Function?

Some people might object to this characterization of corporate management. After all, Wall Street does care about who is leading a company, and different CEOs have different track records. Some CEOs seem to drive their company into the ground and others seem to have a golden touch. I would point out, though, that while there are some bad business strategies (like the ones Devon Banks implemented), most CEOs have been the beneficiaries or victims of a combination of chance events outside anyone's control and the actual work of those unrecognized employees who do a lot of the actual development and production in the company. Consider the fact that CEOs of multinational conglomerates don't really seem to have any meaningful advice for others to follow in their footsteps. Don Geiss's advice for all corporate emergencies is simply "Avoid the Noid" ("Larry King"). Sure he's a fictional character (Geiss, not just the Noid), but is his advice any more helpful than the kind of advice that the actual former GE CEO Jack Welch dispenses, like "Accept change" or "Face reality"? (Heck, he proves my point by encouraging people to manage less and get out of the way.)

Management doesn't have to be superfluous to a company's functioning, but it often is. Many companies have become too big to manage. To start with, the bigger it is, the more tempting it is to turn over responsibility to the corporate structure and let GE (through all of its policies and unrecognized employees) do all the work. To grow beyond a certain point, companies need capital investment, but that means turning to financiers who become partners or owners in the business. Someone with a real love of engineering might have started GE, but eventually the business was handed over to someone from the outside, who had the money the company needed to grow. Such financiers come with one goal—to make money—and that goal can slowly squeeze out all the other goals a company might have.

We think it strange for Jack to be VP of both a television and a microwave division, but at the top of GE is someone who runs a company that not only produces television shows and appliances, but also produces weapons, offers investment services, and makes an assortment of other products. No one human being could understand all of those businesses. Instead we have top-level suits who seem to understand none of them, except in terms of how they make or lose money. Even lower-level managers are having a tougher time keeping track of everything. NBC Universal contains NBC, SyFy, Bravo, and who knows what else. Could any one person have a sense of the diverse target audiences for all those networks?

Ironically, this particular phenomenon is something Adam Smith (1723–1790)—who, despite what you may think, was a professor of philosophy not economics—seems to attack in his *Wealth of Nations*. Admittedly, in that book Smith is attacking government intervention in eighteenth-century businesses, but much of what he says seems applicable to corporations today. Smith argues against government regulation, stating that "what is the species of domestic industry which his capital can employ, and of which the produce is likely to be of the greatest value, every individual, it is evident, can, in his local situation, judge much better than any statesman or lawgiver can do for him."[1] In other words, there is a great danger in relying on someone in the capital telling you how to sell your grain. The problem with regulation is not simply that it limits freedom (Smith is okay with some government regulation). The problem is that people who make the regulations don't know what they're talking about, and wind up doing more harm than good. Is that any different from the modern conglomerate where someone like Jack tells his employees how to write their sketches? (This is a guy who's trying to study comedy by watching episodes of *Friends*.)

As we've seen, modern corporations are so big that they necessarily create distance between those in charge and those taking action. They even exhibit the "presumption and folly" that Smith regards as the greatest danger, as corporations and their employees don't appear to be that concerned about their ignorance. Jack seems to be an exception, but he's also following Six Sigma principles. It boggles the mind that executives have to be told that it's a good management strategy to know how your division works. Of course, even if they tried, the very size of the corporation makes such knowledge impossible at the top levels of the corporation. Instead, we have the equivalent of eighteenth-century kings and ministers ruling the fiefdom of GE. It's worth bearing in mind that the modern conglomerate is probably closer in size to an eighteenth-century nation than it is to an eighteenth-century company.

We can be appalled or perplexed at the way corporations treat television comedy and microwave appliances as interchangeable, but this attitude is just reflective of a larger issue in the modern multinational corporation. The interchangeability of people, lack of interest in anything about a company other than its profitability, and reluctance to take decisive action are all symptoms of a company so big that it has a mind of its own (and not one that anyone can control). This is going to be a problem for any large organization; its workings exceed the human capacity for comprehension. Consider, for example, the United States government. Where else would you find someone responsible for both "extreme weather preparedness and the war on the poor" ("Cooter")?

As we can see from Smith's criticism, the problems we have with companies like GE aren't something inherent to all forms of capitalism. These problems are the result of the way we've been practicing capitalism in the developed world for the last century or two. There's no reason a person can't take pleasure in doing a job, like writing comedies, and also get paid for it. And there's no reason corporations can't strive to make profits. But if an employee's only goal is to get paid and the corporation's only goal is to turn a profit, we can expect more trouble than a Jenna/Tracy feud but without all the fun.

NOTES

1. Adam Smith, *An Inquiry into the Nature and Causes of the Wealth of Nations, Volume I* (Indianapolis, IN: Liberty Fund, 1984), book iv, chapter 2, paragraph 10.

THE EMANCIPATION CORPORATION: LOVING AND LOATHING THE SHINEHARDT WIGS OF THE WORLD

Nicolas Michaud

Jack Donaghy loves his corporation. He loves GE even more than, say, a beloved cookie jar. He respects, cherishes, and even seeks to take care of his beloved corporation. One wonders what he gets out of the deal. Certainly, the corporation can't love Jack in return. GE itself can't actually be concerned with Jack's welfare, can it? The contemporary philosopher Peter French might argue differently. Okay, French may not believe that corporations can love, but he does believe that corporations have a kind of personhood. They're more than just CEOs, workers, and money; they have a kind of personality. So, perhaps, Jack's love is not so misplaced after all.

One worry, though, comes to mind. If Jack's emotions are appropriate, and French's reasoning isn't misguided, then corporations have a kind of a mind of their own—a mind that we use to do our will. Granted, it's often true that we don't require much from a corporation—but we could. When corporations break the law, we try to force them to change their ways. And as we shall see, GE, the object of Jack's love, is a kind of slave, born into bondage—if it is a person.

GE: Man, Machine, or Martian?

So what reason do we have to believe that corporations can actually be persons? In his book *Corporate Ethics*, French argues that corporations have what we call "actorship." This actorship means that corporations have a kind of will. In the way that you and I can will a particular end to come to pass, so can corporations. Without any one person making the decision, a corporation can act on its own. There's no one person who's essential to running a corporation. Even without Jack, or even without CEO Don Geiss, GE would continue. While both Jack and Don are useful, they could (and will eventually) be replaced.

Corporations can even act against the will of the CEO Such actions often can't be traced to any single person in the corporation. One example of this kind of phenomenon is the explosion of the Space Shuttle *Challenger*. No one at NASA wanted the space shuttle to explode. Oddly enough, though, many people knew that the shuttle was in danger and not good for launch. How could the shuttle have been launched anyway? We could simply blame the director of NASA, but that would miss the point. He didn't want the space shuttle to explode, nor was it solely his fault. French thinks this is an example of how a corporation can move on its own, even in ways contrary to the individual wills of the people within it.

Central to the way corporations make decisions is not the mind of one CEO, but instead, the corporate internal decision structure (CID). The CID structure is the summation of the statement of purpose, the culture of the corporation, the decisions of the stockholders and CEO, as well as the rule structure that governs the business of a particular corporation. All of these things together are something like the mind of the corporation, which can act against the will of any one particular person. Think of it like this: the corporation at GE can decide to fire Jack. This is clearly against his will and it may also not be something that any individual really wants to do. Don likes Jack, but by himself, Don can't make every decision; GE itself has substantial control over Jack's fate. The CID structure mandates what is best for the corporation.

It helps if we have an idea of what it means to be an actor in this context. Jack Donaghy, for example, has three things that French believes are essential to actorship: one, intentionality; two, the ability to make rational decisions; and three, the ability to change behaviors in response to external events. Jack has plans, has intentionality, including his intention to become the CEO of GE. He makes plans in order to achieve this end, and competes with Devon Banks to prevent Devon from becoming CEO. Jack also makes rational business decisions on a regular basis—like his Trivection oven. Rational decision making doesn't need to be brilliant. Even Jenna makes rational decisions—they may not be the brightest decisions, but they're the result of a process of rational thought. And Jack is able to change behaviors in response to events. When he wants to become CEO, he decides to get rid of his collection of cookie jars. Not only does this demonstrate planning and intentionality, but it also demonstrates that Jack can change his behavior in response to what's going on around him. Can the same be said for a corporation?

Peter French thinks so. He argues that corporations can make plans and thereby demonstrate intentionality, make rational decisions, and change their behaviors in response to external events. We might think that GE's actions are the result of one CEO's decisions, but this isn't quite correct. Corporations don't act on the decisions of the CEO alone. The corporation is a conglomeration of component parts and its decisions are the result of those parts working together. We aren't so different.

We consider ourselves actors in the philosophical sense, even though we're made up of component parts that work together to come to particular decisions. The human beings who make up a corporation's CID structure are not so dissimilar from the neurons that make up a human being's brain.

Jack and GE Sitting in a Tree, K-I-S-S-I-N-G!

All right, so perhaps Jack isn't completely insane in showering his affections on a corporation. If French is correct—and he does have some good evidence—then a corporation has a kind of basic personhood. When we create corporations, we might literally be making actors. But this is a real problem. Actors are not just things that exhibit French's three criteria. They can also be praised and blamed for the things they do. Think about it like this: if a corporation is no different as a tool from, say, a Funcooker, then it would be silly to thank it for a job well done. If, on the other hand, corporations are actors, similar to you and me, then they can be praised or blamed for their actions, as those actions are the result of rational and intentional behavior.

The ability to praise and blame corporations is useful. Sometimes, like in the case of NASA, we cannot seem to find one person who is solely responsible for the action of the corporation—it seems almost as if the corporation acted of its own will. If we want to blame GE for an immoral act and we realize that neither Jack nor Don is by himself responsible, we may rationally blame the corporation as a whole. But if a corporation can be the object of rational blame, then it's the kind of thing that ought to be treated with some dignity. And if that's right, then a corporation is part of our "moral community." It may well have a right to the same basic respect that members of the moral community deserve.

Marvin T. Brown, a philosopher who specializes in business ethics, thinks that treating corporations as members of our moral community leads to some very strange conclusions. Brown points out that French's theory results in the conclusion that we've enslaved corporations. If a corporation is an actor and part of the moral community, then we're forcing an intentional and rational being to do our will. Imagine what this does to Jack! His beloved corporation is a slave!

But the fact that it seems silly to consider corporations as slaves doesn't make it untrue. So far, French's argument looks rather compelling and leads to an uncomfortable conclusion—that corporations are our slaves. Under most circumstances we're in agreement, I'm sure, that enslavement is wrong. Corporations can make highly rational decisions and make plans farther into the future than most animals, perhaps even farther than most human beings. The fact that we don't like this implication of French's view just isn't a sufficient reason to reject it. Arguments don't always result in conclusions that we like.

Marxists have spoken about slavery and corporations for some time, calling those who work for corporations "wage slaves." These workers aren't slaves in the traditional sense. They're slaves to work—to earning a wage—and are unable to express their creative will in their labor (something Marx regarded as crucial for human flourishing). They're stuck, pouring their creative energy into a corporation that cares little for them. They're forced to do the will of the corporation, regardless of their own wills, in order to make ends meet. Ironically, if French is correct, GE is also a slave, and Jack is a small component part of that slave. The workers are enslaved to the corporation and the corporation is also a slave—but to whom?

As it turns out, the corporations are enslaved to the same people that the workers are enslaved to—the stockholders. A corporation must do the will of the stockholder, as do Don Geiss, Jack Donaghy, Liz Lemon, and the other employees all the way to the bottom. The corporation itself and the blue-collar workers are far more enslaved than the CEO. Liz can quit and find other work, but those working in the mailroom or filling cups of coffee for minimum wage may not have this option. And as for the corporation itself, it cannot choose to disappoint the stockholders without severe consequences. The stockholders hold all of the metaphorical keys and they can even kill the corporation if they so choose.

It's *Alive* . . . Kill It!

How should we treat GE and other corporations, then? Should we pity them? Or should we ignore them in the same way that we ignore other wage slaves? Should we tell them all that they are lucky to have work at all and order them to stop bitching? Well, there is at least one significant difference between human wage slaves and the corporation. Human beings are not really designed by other human beings in the way that corporations are. Granted, we raise humans and we educate them, and on occasion, brainwash them, but they're still hardwired in particular ways that we can't really get around. Corporations, though, are the result of our direct design. The CID structure is specifically designed by human beings in most regards. The CEO decides how the culture of the corporation will work, the stockholders create the purpose and rules of the corporation, and the various bosses within the corporation design the policies and procedures that dictate how the corporation will act.

Given this difference, it's clear that while wage slavery is wrong because it violates an actor's will and uses that actor as just a piece of machinery to line some stockholder's pockets, the creation of corporate slaves is even more twisted. While wage slavery is probably just wrong, the creation of actors for the purpose of being unquestioning slaves is insidious. Granted, we can't argue that the corporations are being forced to do things against their will: the CID structure is designed so that they *want* to do the will of the stockholders, and only the stockholders! GE, regardless of the impact on any of its workers or its customers, will do whatever is necessary to make the stockholders as much money as possible. We feel absolved of using corporations as slaves by arguing that the corporations *want* to do our will; the irony is that we *designed* them to do our will.

So now we have the classic problem of the willing slave. If we talked with Jack, he would have no problem with this. Clearly, the purpose of business is to make money, and if we have to create a corporate slave in order to do this, then so be it. The answer is probably not that easy, though, because not only have we created slaves but we've created slaves that are willing to destroy themselves in order to please their masters. If Jack truly loves GE as much as he seems to, then even he should balk at this realization.

In the United States, corporations regularly commit a kind of suicide in order to make massive profits for the stockholders. Despite the fact that this results in great harm for everyone else who has a stake in the corporation (stakeholders)—like the consumers, workers, CEO, and the community—the corporation has no choice but to do the will of its master. Corporations regularly allow themselves to be bought out or make decisions that will result in massive amounts of money made in the short term but will result in the collapse of the corporation in the long term. They are programmed to commit a kind of corporate suicide when it suits the stockholders.

Where's Kenneth? We Need to Blame *Someone*!

Corporations are like computers. They are highly intelligent programs designed for a particular purpose. For this reason, corporations are willing to do things that even harm themselves in order to meet this very basic program. We would hope that if Jack truly loves GE, he would seek to change this. It seems shortsighted to create an entity that will follow one basic rule to the point of its own destruction. Beyond this, because we program no ethical rules into the corporation, corporations are usually willing to do things we consider extremely unethical to meet their basic program. And that's why corporations are often so willing to do things that harm human beings. The CID structure is purposely made by the stockholders to exclude ethics because ethics gets in the way of making profit. So now we realize that when we create corporations, we're creating actors—but actors without any sense of ethics and without any aversion to doing harm to human beings.

When a corporation does something unethical, it seems unreasonable just to blame someone like Don Geiss, as he doesn't have total control of how the corporation acts; it's not just a simple extension of his will. As a matter of fact, the corporate action may be against Don's will. Given this, who do we have to blame for a corporation burying toxic waste next to a school, selling cars that explode, or covering up dangerous side effects of corporate products? Do we just blame the corporation?

We usually want to find human beings to blame for corporate evils, but because we cannot locate any one human who is responsible, we are rationally forced to blame the corporation as a whole. But this doesn't do any good. After all, corporations can't feel bad or ashamed about their actions. Yet if I'm right, and corporations are a kind of slave to the stockholders, and are acting because they were designed to act the way they do, then we do have someone to blame for corporate evils—those of us who design corporations to act in these ways. And we, the supporters of the free market, are blameworthy for the actions of these corporations because we support this design of the system and the corporations. Every time a corporation does something unethical, it does so because we design or at least support a system that makes it such. We're the people who support this system of slavery, and so we're the true key holders and we're the ones who should take the blame the next time GE puts out something incredibly stupid—like the Tracy Jordan Meat Machine.

LIZ AND JACK CAN'T BE FRIENDS!: COMMUNITARIANISM, LIBERTARIANISM, AND POLITICS AT *30 ROCK*

Nicolas Michaud

I like you. You have the boldness of a much younger woman.

—Jack Donaghy to Liz Lemon (Pilot)

Liz Lemon's friendship with Jack Donaghy is impossible. They're so different from each other that there's no way they should be able to stand being in the same room. Liz tries to be a people person, invests herself in her staff, and sometimes seems rather anticapitalism. Jack, on the other hand, is greedy and selfish—the poster-boy for the triumph of the free market. How is it that these two people are capable of being such fast friends? Is this just another example of our televisions selling us something that doesn't work nearly as well as it seems—like the Tracy Jordan Meat Machine? The very philosophies that Liz and Jack live by cannot coexist—they're incompatible! *30 Rock* may well be feeding us another line of bull. Before revolting, though, let's explore Liz's and Jack's philosophies of life and find out for ourselves if there is any way to bring them together. If so, then, I suppose, we'll owe *30 Rock* an apology.

Liz is basically a communitarian, insofar as she believes in taking care of her community. Jack is a libertarian, with an every-man-for-himself mentality. Well, if we wanted this chapter to be very short, I could simply point out that virtually no philosopher believes that communitarianism and libertarianism are compatible and leave it at that. Liz and Jack's friendship seems far-fetched. There's little reason to think that a philosophy based on working together for the greater good of the community—communitarianism—and a philosophy built around independence and self-promotion—libertarianism—could go hand in hand.

All right, I'll be generous. Let's consider it from a different perspective: maybe the fact that we can imagine Liz and Jack being friends is reason for us to have hope about libertarianism and communitarianism. Liz and Jack do seem to find some common ground. Granted, initially, Liz couldn't stand Jack, and Jack was only using Liz. But as time has gone on, they have found agreements and common ground. Perhaps, then, we can use this as a starting point for libertarianism and communitarianism.

"I Wolfed My Teamster Sub for You!" —Liz

Let's have a closer look at these two philosophies. Communitarians believe that the community comes first. They believe that, in order for us to create a great society, we must give up our selfishness and, instead, seek to benefit the community as a whole. Each person, then, must do what's in everyone else's best interest, as well as their own. The communitarian rationale is that we all benefit most from a society that focuses on "positive rights"—rights that don't just tell us what the government can't do to us, but what it *will* do *for* us. So, for example, not only should the government be prevented from killing off its citizens, it should also do things to improve the lives of its citizens (like providing health care, housing, and education, for example).

Communitarians such as the philosopher Charles Taylor believe that our communities are essential to who we are— they are essential to our "personhood." The communities in which we're raised—including families, churches, schools, peer groups, countries, and so on—help make us who we are. Communities, or combinations of them, constitute our identities—they make us who we are. When you think about this, it may seem a bit hippy-dippy, at least at first. But consider trying to exit a community that's important to you—your family, your friends, or your church—and reject it completely. This is extremely difficult to do, and it could be harmful. It could lead to severe depression or an identity crisis.

Liz is not a "super" communitarian, but that's okay. Communitarianism needn't be socialism or communism. In fact, most communitarians prefer a moderate path and focus largely on avoiding what they believe to be the extreme of libertarianism. Liz often seeks to help others; she fights for community-oriented goals. Her show, and the people who make it up, are essential to who she is. And despite her own tendencies toward selfishness, she often seeks to separate herself from the remarkably narcissistic and egotistical behavior of those around her. Consider, for example, when she wants to prevent an annoying man from having a hot dog: she buys all of them. A libertarian would probably have found a way to make money off the hot dogs, once having purchased them. Liz, instead, uses them to benefit her coworkers—she seeks to do things to help her community. Granted, she is not extreme in this regard, but neither are most communitarians.

"I Have Faith . . . in Things I Can See and Buy and Deregulate. Capitalism Is My Religion." —Jack

Libertarians, on the other hand, see little or no value in helping the community. In fact, libertarians believe that when we try to help others, we're actually demeaning them. In a libertarian world, we should avoid infringing on other people's rights, but there's no reason to do extra things for them. Things like health care are things you receive if you work hard enough; this lack of charity provides incentive and self-respect.

Libertarians value cold, hard freedom. They don't want to be forced to share. If they're going to share, it'll be because they choose to. Libertarians focus heavily on the negative rights—rights that prohibit things from being done to us, but don't force us to do anything. Libertarians believe that positive rights infringe on negative rights. If someone has a positive right to health care, then we're probably forcing someone else (many people, in fact) to help pay for that health care. And to a libertarian, forcing people to share in order to help the community is just theft.

Central to the libertarian philosophy is the idea that we're all on our own. We are intrinsically independent. We don't actually need others or a community, and we basically make ourselves who we are. Notice how this connects to the idea that we do damage to others if we try to help them. Not only are we playing Robin Hood by stealing from rich members of the community to help poor members, but we're also treating the people we're "helping" as if they're unable to help themselves. By doing this, we create people who are dependent on the system and vulnerable to it.

Jack is very clearly libertarian. His notions of self-power and independence lead him to a deep belief in capitalism and the corporate system. He believes in pulling himself up by his own bootstraps—and succeeding on his own. He doesn't want to be forced to help anyone else in the community, and he has no problem using other people to achieve his goals. For Jack, then, an idea like providing everyone health care is repulsive. Not only is it stealing from him but, also, it assumes that other people wouldn't be able to make it on their own. By doing this, it denies these people the ability to self-create.

"Are These People Your Family? Why Are They All Smiling? Who's Being Ostracized?" —Jack

Now we can see why it's so difficult to imagine how Liz and Jack get along. Not only do they have different ideas about how government should work, but they have radically different philosophical perspectives generally. Communitarianism and libertarianism seem incompatible. But is it possible for these two philosophies to come together? Well, Liz and Jack manage to do it, and if that isn't just more baloney, then there might be hope. Maybe we can have our health care and refuse it too.

Over the course of their friendship, Jack comes to care for Liz, and Liz learns to appreciate Jack. This may be the first step toward bringing these two philosophies together. Perhaps a level of moderation is necessary. If Liz is not too communitarian and Jack is not too libertarian, then maybe they can get along. But this is a bit of a cop-out. In bringing any two philosophies together, compromises will be necessary. But this doesn't resolve the major tension. Communitarians believe that the community makes us who we are, and libertarians believe we make ourselves who we are.

So the question of whether our community is essential to who we are becomes the first question that must be resolved. We can see the glimmer of an answer in the friendship between Liz and Jack. First, the fact that Jack doesn't just use Liz to get what he wants is a bit of a clue. He's not a man alone. Jack's relationship with his mother is also an important key. Jack's mother profoundly affects him and, although not for the best, her impact has helped make him who he is. He's not just a self-made man. In his desire to become his own person, Jack seeks to distance himself from, and prove himself to, his mother. Even Jack's own corporation is essential to him. GE is the corporation that gave him a chance to become the man he is. He is proud of his accomplishment and he wouldn't have succeeded had it not been for the company, which is also a community.

No one is entirely self-made, not even Jack Donaghy. Perhaps it's true that dependence on, or blind obedience to, any one person or entity is problematic, but there's good reason to believe that we need others and our communities. When a person emigrates from one country to another, she takes her culture with her and usually seeks others who understand that culture. And if a person is required to leave his language, culture, and heritage behind, this often harms him. The communities in which we're raised continue to be a huge part of who we are. Even people who decide to leave the religion of their youth largely define themselves by opposing themselves to those beliefs. We cannot just forget the communities that make us who we are, or ignore them; those communities (or our opposition to them) define us.

Jack is a prime example of someone who claims to need no one, but depends on others at every turn. This seems to be a major flaw of libertarianism. We're not entirely self-made and our communities are very important to who we are. For all of Jack's claims to the contrary, he needs others and benefits greatly from his participation in the GE community. Without it, Jack suffers. When Devon forces Jack to leave GE, Jack cannot stay away long. He's willing to take a job as a mail clerk in order to remain part of his beloved community. This is good evidence for the communitarian claim that our communities are extremely important to us.

So one important step toward reconciling communitarianism and libertarianism has been taken. Even a super free market advocate, like Jack, is made and enabled by his relationships with others. To assume that we're entirely self-made just seems contrary to the facts. We're defined by our communities (or at least in opposition to them). Realizing this, we can begin to ease up on the libertarian belief that the help of others harms all people—Jack is certainly helped by Liz on numerous occasions (acting, anyone?). Help is often necessary for success, and it's through our communities that we begin to achieve self-empowerment. We needn't worry that by helping the community we're doing harm to the individual. In fact, the individual is empowered by, and often needs, the community.

"I Truly Don't Like You as a Person. Can't One Human Being Not Like Another Human Being? Can't We All Just Not Get Along?" —Liz

Communitarianism has a significant flaw. Consider the application of the communitarian philosophy—we should do what's best for the community as a whole. While this comes from the idea that our communities are essential to who we are, the idea is actually based on the welfare of the individual. For example, while Liz attempts to do what's best for the *TGS* community, she often still seems selfish and self-absorbed. This may be due to the simple fact that even when we attempt to benefit the community, one motivating factor is our own individual welfare.

Valuing the community involves valuing the individual. Communitarians argue that we should be invested in the community because it's essential to our selfhood, but this only makes sense if I value my self. One of my primary values is my self, and this provides a reason for valuing those things that I identify with my welfare—family, friends, communities, and so on.

Jack: Lemon, I'm impressed. You're beginning to think like a businessman.

Liz: A businesswoman.

Jack: I don't think that's a word.

From this point, we might be able to follow Liz and Jack's example and bring communitarianism and libertarianism together. Both communitarianism and libertarianism value individual people. Liz wants what's best for herself, as does Jack. The fundamental question is this: what's the best way for us to do what's in our best interest?

As we recognized earlier, our community is essential to who we are. And as we have accepted that one motivating force behind both theories is the welfare of the individual, now we can seek to do what is in the individual's best interest. Obviously, Jack's estrangement from others, like his mother, isn't in his best interest, but his relationship with Liz and the community of GE is. So much so, in fact, that without these relationships, he loses himself. It would be wise, then, for the libertarian to accept the importance of the community to his own well-being.

Liz and Jack exemplify this merging of philosophies. Liz, over the course of the show, comes to realize the power of individual motivation, desire, and self-preservation. To ignore the fact that we're highly motivated by our own best interest isn't realistic. Jack, on the other hand, learns how important his community is to him—he isn't an island. To allow damage to be done to his community is to allow damage to be done to himself. Clearly, then, the goal becomes to benefit and support the community, but it just so happens that this also maximizes the success of the individual. Jack's dog-eat-dog mentality only seems to work as long as there's a community structure that supports it. This mentality may simply not be in Jack's best interest, or in ours, as exemplified each time Jack attempts to turn his personal relationships into matters of pure business.

Liz and Jack need each other. Realizing this, we see that communitarianism only makes sense if we value each individual, and libertarianism only makes sense if we do what is actually in the best interest of the individual—value the community. Communitarianism is only rational insofar as it doesn't allow harm to be done to the individuals who constitute the community, and libertarianism can only achieve its goal of maximizing the success of the individual by recognizing the necessary role that community plays in the welfare of the individual. Liz and Jack have found an effective way to bring their two philosophies together through rational compromise. Perhaps philosophers could learn a thing or two from their relationship. So it turns out that my original claim was false—Liz and Jack's friendship isn't impossible—it might even be necessary.

Now as far as my apology goes, I'm holding out for a refund on my Tracy Jordan Meat Machine.

PART FOUR

MIND GRAPES
(TO NOURISH YOUR
THINKING)

"THE BUBBLE," THE CAVE, AND *SAMSARA*: BEING DELUDED AT *30 ROCK*

Adam Barkman

"It's the bubble," says Liz Lemon to her boss, Jack Donaghy, about her boyfriend Dr. Andrew ("Drew") Baird. "He's a doctor who doesn't know the Heimlich maneuver; he can't cook; he's bad at sex; but he has no idea."

"That's the danger of being super-handsome," replies Jack. "When you're in the bubble, no one ever tells you the truth." This episode continues with Liz determined to burst Drew's bubble and save him from living "a lie," but it ends with the two of them breaking up because, as it turns out, Drew doesn't "like it outside the bubble." In the closing scene, a sad fact becomes clear: some people prefer delusions to reality.

Yet this isn't some new revelation. According to a number of major philosophical and religious traditions—not the least of which are Platonism and Hinduism—most people, both in reality and on *30 Rock*, choose some form of delusion or illusion over truth and reality.

Illusion and Reality

Although Hinduism has its roots in the polytheistic traditions of Persia, its modern form dates back about three thousand years to the time of the Upanishads: needless to say, it's older than Devon Banks's Church of Practicology!

According to the Upanishadic worldview, life, as most people experience it, is inextricably linked with suffering. For every pleasure a person experiences, there is a corresponding pain, and this isn't resolved by the apparent fact that when a person dies, his soul, shaped by *karma* (or the ethical choices made in this life), is reincarnated to a higher or lower life form within the cycle of life and death known as *samsara*. Even the gods and goddesses, such as Shiva and Indra, exist within *samsara* (albeit in its highest heaven) and as such still experience pleasure and pain.

The Hindus were the first proponents of what I'll call "negative happiness," or happiness as the absence of suffering.[1] For the Hindus—as for the Buddha (ca. 563–ca. 483 BCE) later on—pain is to be eliminated, though often it needs to be increased first. But how does a person end suffering?

Hindus believe that suffering arises out of ignorance, in particular, ignorance of Reality. An individual suffers to the extent that he believes he is separate from the one true reality. Delusion condemns such an individual to continued reincarnation: *samsara* itself, with its *karma*, heavens, hells, reincarnation, NBCs, and *TGS*s, is the problem.

The enlightened individual, therefore, knows Reality, which is to say that through meditation and spiritual exercise, he comes to see that at his core he is *not* an individual self at all. Rather, his individual self, his *Atman*, is one with *Brahman*, or Ultimate Reality. Thus, the enlightened individual realizes both that everything that is not soul is illusion (*maya*), and that everything that thinks it is an individual soul, though not itself an illusion, is trapped in the illusion of *samsara*. In this way, a person is happy when he achieves *moksha*, freedom from all illusions and delusions.

The most famous Greek philosopher, Plato (ca. 428–348 BCE), would have agreed with Hinduism on a number of these points. In particular, Plato would have applauded Hinduism's emphasis on knowledge and reality over and against delusion and illusion. Plato's most famous discussion of these notions can be found in his allegory of the cave, which goes something like this:

Imagine a cave inhabited by prisoners who have been chained and immobile since their earliest days: "their legs and necks tied up in a way which keeps them in one place and allows them to look only straight ahead to the back of the cave wall which is in front of them."[2] Behind the prisoners is a huge fire, and between the fire and the prisoners is a raised walkway, along which people walk carrying things on their heads, including artifacts of people and animals. The prisoners can watch only the shadows cast by the men, and so they don't know that they are just shadows, nor are they aware that the echoes they hear are just echoes. The prisoners would mistake the shadows for the real things and the echoes for the real sounds; they would confuse illusions for reality, since illusion is all they have ever seen or heard.

Now suppose a prisoner got free, stood up, and was shown the real things. This prisoner wouldn't recognize the real things for what they are, and might maintain the delusion that the shadows and the echo are more real. Moreover, if this prisoner were to gaze at the fire, he might be struck blind by it and would quickly turn back to the shadows on the wall, toward what he can see clearly and to what he believes to be real. He might, in short, prefer a delusion to the truth. However, if someone were forcibly to drag him (in a Liz-dragging-Tracy manner) upward, out of the cave and into the sunlight, the prisoner, though initially angry and totally overwhelmed by the brightness of reality, would eventually come to see that nothing that he once believed was true, and now, in the face of truth, he would see that the Sun is not only the source of all life, regularity, and structure, but is also "the ultimate cause of all those things he and his fellow prisoners had been seeing."[3]

For Plato, the cave represents the world of nonbeing and becoming—worlds of flux and illusion. The prisoners are people who are deluded into thinking that these illusory worlds are Reality. The fire, as a reflection of the Sun, truly helps people to see, but if people are used to the darkness, they'll shun the fire's light and revelation. The fire itself finds its source in the Sun, which represents Ultimate Reality—the world of Forms or the eternal, unchanging world of Truth and Goodness, which are the source of, and giver of meaning to, all things. Those who are led to the truth (those led out of the cave) will be angry at first, but once they realize the true nature of the Sun, they will no longer wish to be prisoners and will find happiness basking in the Sun's rays.

Despite their broad agreement, we can see that Plato and Hinduism disagree on at least two matters. First, Plato maintains we have an essential self and a given nature that is identical neither to other souls nor to Reality itself. Hinduism disagrees. Second, Plato says Truth and Morality belong to Reality; and their opposites, falsity and immorality, belong to the world of nonbeing. Hinduism insists that true and false opinions and moral and immoral choices, insofar as they are in the soul, are equally part of Brahman, or Reality.

Hinduism and Platonism agree on three key points: that this world isn't Reality but is an imperfect reflection of Reality (Plato) or an illusion (Hinduism), that knowledge embraced will lead people from delusions and illusions to Reality, and that people will be happy when they find Reality. With all this in mind, let's look at the folks at *30 Rock*.

"I Want to Use 'Ironic' However I Want"

This chapter began with a reference to Liz's boyfriend Drew and his preference for the "bubble" of delusion over reality. So now let's scrutinize him a bit further.

Drew's delusions spring from the privileges people give him as a result of his good looks. Among the benefits of his good looks are that they put people in a good mood (as in the case of the heterosexual police officer who didn't ticket Drew); they offer potential financial rewards (as when Calvin Klein offered Drew an underwear modeling gig); and they inspire in both women and men alike the hope of dating him (for instance, when the gay men and straight women at the tennis court either gave him their court or let him win). Drew, in short, is treated differently than others because he has something that others don't have. As a result, he can't understand how most people live: this is the reality that he's chosen to remain deluded about. It's hardly surprising, then, that he tells Liz, "I want to use 'ironic' however I want" ("The Bubble").

Both Plato and the Hindus would have a problem with Drew for a number of reasons. First, he (and others around him) overvalue physical appearance. According to both Hinduism and Platonism, the physical world is largely an illusion and as such it, and all that belongs to it, including physical appearances, are of little (Platonism) or no (Hinduism) importance. Second, although attention was drawn to his delusions ("Drew," Liz tells him, "I'm going to tell you this for your own good"), Drew still prefers to live in the ignorance of *samsara* and in the familiarity of the shadowy cave rather than in the light of reality. Third, like the prisoners of *samsara* or the cave, Drew erroneously thinks he's "happy this way."

"That's Not the Way I Remember It"

Liz has two major delusions, the first of which is thinking she's nicer than she really is. For instance, in at least two episodes, she had flashbacks about the past wherein she "remembered," in the first case, having been a supportive friend to Jenna ("The Rural Juror") and in the second case, having been a harmless nerd who was picked on in high school ("Reunion"). But as it turns out, she remembered wrongly in both cases. In the first instance, she remembered herself as more supportive (and cooler) than she was, and in the second, she discovered that she was in fact a bully "who made high school a living hell for everyone." Moreover, in both cases, when Liz's false memory was brought to her attention, she used her sense of humor to brush it off "instead of dealing with [things] in a real way" ("Reunion"). That is, not only did she initially choose to block old memories and create false ones, but she continued to support this project by laughing about it as if it weren't important and hence wasn't something that needed to be rectified. Nowadays this would be called a defense mechanism, but neither Plato nor the Hindus would excuse such emotional or instinctual behavior for distorting reality: knowledge should lead people to reality; it shouldn't be buried and reburied with laughter because people are too emotionally weak to deal with it. Take that, Liz Lemon!

Liz's second delusion—that she can "really have it all" (that is, a deeply satisfying job, a fulfilling personal life, and marriage)—is a delusion shared by many modern women (and men) and one wonderfully explored in *30 Rock*, as well as in this book. This delusion has two parts: the belief that work is all Liz needs at the moment and the belief that one day she will have a utopian balance of work and family life.

Liz is "single and pretend[s] to be happy about it," as Jack says, and although Liz doesn't always see her own delusion in this regard, viewers are aware of it and indeed recognize that the show is making an important comment about the way things really are. Most people naturally (in the Platonic sense of each thing having a given nature) need intimacy—hence, Jack isn't so far off when he indicates that even being "groped on the subway" might be good for Liz ("Blind Date"). Most people (save for the few who have dedicated themselves solely to the attainment of enlightenment) will live, all things considered, happier lives if they are married. We see Liz, denying the reality that she's a single, middle-aged woman whose window of opportunity for marriage is closing rapidly, constantly telling herself that she has "time" and that she'll just buy a wedding dress now and use it "when [she gets] married" ("SeinfeldVision"). Liz deludes herself into thinking that her work is enough to satisfy her at the moment. She denies, at least implicitly, the reality that now—right now—she is still a person who has the same intimacy needs as other human beings.

Besides the delusion of work being satisfying enough for her at the moment, Liz also fails, in her utopian dream, to recognize the reality that a good marriage requires give and take. By definition a person can't have everything his or her way and still treat his or her partner with the selflessness proper to a healthy marriage. This notion is amplified when children are added to the equation, and in this it becomes crystal clear that Liz is misguided in her plan to work sixty- to seventy-hour workweeks and still raise a child. Viewers, of course, see the irony of Liz thinking that she can do this and hence draw the correct conclusion, namely, that the "you can have it all" attitude is one of the greatest modern delusions of all.

"For Men It's Called a 'Hardy Boy'"

As the protagonist of *30 Rock*, Jack isn't typically thought of as delusional, yet he prefers certain illusions to reality. Besides once having been in the same bubble of delusion as Drew—that is, the delusion brought on by good looks ("The Bubble")—Jack is delusional about the merits of capitalism ("St. Valentine's Day"), the merits of the Republican Party ("Goodbye, My Friend"), the merits of American imperialism

("Cougars"), his own creative ideas and artistic ability ("Jack the Writer"), and his own morality ("The C-Word"). This book only has so many pages; I'll just have to focus on the last two delusions.

As for being deluded about his own creative ideas and artistic ability, in two episodes in season one Jack decides to sit in with the writers of *TGS* to see how they come up with their ideas for skits. Jack, however, begins to add his own ideas to the mix, all of which are terrible, frustrating the writers. Predictably, Jack is clueless about this, believing not only that he has great ideas but that everyone is enjoying having him at the meetings. Only when Liz finally snaps and tells him that he can't sit in on the meetings anymore does Jack get the point. Moreover, in the follow-up episode, a similar scenario takes place, but this time with Jack being delusional about his acting abilities.

Both of these cases are pretty clear-cut examples of delusion being brought on by ignorance and overcome by knowledge. That is, both present Hindu or Platonic readings of delusion and its remedy. What is most interesting, though, is how they lead into Jack's other delusion, namely, his false sense of his own morality. For instance, after Jack's delusions are revealed to him in the skit episode, he wakes up to the reality of his own shortcomings in regard to creativity. Not knowing how to handle being told that his suggestions are unwanted and that he is bad at something, Jack takes refuge in himself—not in the sense of genuine confidence in knowing his own objective worth (as Plato might say) or in the sense of realizing that he is *Atman* and *Brahman* (as the Hindus would maintain), but rather in his own pride or inordinate superiority to all others, especially those who disagree with him. Consequently, Jack demands Liz apologize for kicking him out of the skit meetings, but his demand is conveyed to her via his assistant, Jonathan, who asks Liz not to mention that Jack wants her to apologize. Pride makes it impossible for Jack not only to apologize for causing the writers such grief but even to ask for an apology from them when he thinks he has been wronged. Jack doesn't know how to be genuinely humble, and this stems from being out of touch with reality. What else would cause him to order a "Nancy Drew," but explain to the bartender that "for men it's called a 'Hardy Boy'"?

"I Can't Handle the Truth!"

Whereas Liz and Jack are subtly delusional in a few respects, Kenneth Parcell is dramatically delusional in many respects. He sees the world as a place where religion has never done any harm ("Christmas Special"), thinks TV is a pure, truth-telling medium ("The C-Word"), and sees everyone living in *Muppets*-like harmony ("Apollo, Apollo"). Indeed, Kenneth's entire worldview—a naive, flawed form of Christianity (whose founder declared himself "the Truth")[4]—is founded on a giant delusion, which is summed up in his own declaration: "I can't handle the truth!" ("Larry King").

It's particularly sad, at least on a Platonic reading, that although many of Kenneth's actions are consistent with reality, his consistency with reality is based on blind faith and not on knowledge. Kenneth does what's right, but he doesn't do it for the right reasons. He's afraid of using his mind to delve deeper into reality and so retreats into the delusion of unexamined dogma.

"No; You Look Younger. . . . You Look Like a Fetus."

Like Kenneth and Drew, Jenna Maroney is unquestionably deluded in a whole host of matters, not the least of which is her overestimation of her own beauty and celebrity.

In two particular episodes, she goes to extreme lengths to keep her true age a secret. In "Jack Meets Dennis," she gets botox and other facial treatments that make her look as young as "a fetus." And in "Jackie Jormp-Jomp," she pretends to be dead to draw attention to herself and her movie. But when a tribute poster revealing her age is about to be unveiled, she quickly "comes back from the dead." Or again, in other episodes, she tells Liz that "love is hiding who you really are at all times—even when you're sleeping" ("Subway Hero"), and she admits, "I've always reminded myself of Grace Kelly" ("Black Tie").

Of course, her delusions about beauty are intimately connected with her belief that celebrity and attention are very important. Thus, we see that she is happy to have her picture in the newspaper, even if she is obese ("The Collection") or passed-out drunk ("The Aftermath"). Additionally, she's proud that her single "Muffin-Top" is number one in Israel of all places ("Jack-Tor"), and wonders, "If [actors] weren't around, how would people know who to vote for?" ("Reunion").

In the end, it's Frank Rossitano, noted hat guru, who voices the Hindu-Platonic assessment of Jenna: "You're a big phony. Everything about you is fake" ("Up All Night").

"Just Be Yourself and I Guarantee You, Every Single Person in This Room Will One Day Be President of the United States!"

Tracy Jordan is an easy target—in many ways too easy to make discussion even worthwhile. For instance, in "Hard Ball," he tells Kenneth, "Okay, that's enough," when Kenneth starts to drop a bunch of truth-bombs on him. Tracy's race-related delusions are of some interest, however, especially as they compare and contrast with other characters' delusions.

To some extent, it's understandable that Tracy, as a member of a minority race, is sensitive about race-related issues. It's hard to fault him for putting *some* value on things like "street cred" ("Jack Meets Dennis"), and we might even feel slightly moved when he advises a graduating class of African American high school students, "Just be yourself and I guarantee you, every single person in this room will one day be president of the United States" ("Kidney Now!").

Nevertheless, Tracy's delusion lies in the fact that he overemphasizes race and sees conspiracies where there aren't any. Consider three examples. First, in the pilot episode, Tracy talks to Liz about *TGS*, saying that the show is a great chance to thwart the evil efforts of "white dudes. . . . All of them," and then goes on to say how these same "white dudes" have been "injecting AIDS into [his] chicken nuggets." Second, Tracy offends the head honcho at NBC, Don Geiss, by falsely implying that he's a racist because there aren't many African Americans at his party ("Corporate Crush"). And third, when Tracy is diagnosed with diabetes, he tells Kenneth, "There is no link between diabetes and diet. That's a white myth, Ken. Like Larry Bird and Colorado" ("Retreat to Move Forward").

Of course, Tracy isn't the only one who is deluded in thinking that race is a bigger issue than it is: Liz talks about her "white guilt" even though she herself did nothing to justify such guilt ("Jack-Tor"). Toofer, who ironically acts more like a WASP than anything, sees even harmless things like dressing up in drag for a comedy skit as demeaning toward black men ("The Break-Up"). And Stephen Black, a black man Liz once dated, thinks that the only reason that a white woman wouldn't want to date him is because she is a "racist" ("The Source Awards").

On a Hindu-Platonic reading, Tracy and the others need proper knowledge about the way things really are so that they don't blow things out of proportion. To turn a blind eye to reality is to embrace ignorance, which, in turn, can only lead a person away from happiness.

The Danger of Thinking "Science Is Whatever We Want It to Be"; or, the Conclusion of the Matter

Most of the characters on *30 Rock*, like most people in general, suffer from one delusion or another. Greater knowledge of, and action in accordance with, reality will ultimately make people happier. Dr. Leo Spaceman, for instance, is deluded and hence will ultimately be more miserable for maintaining that "science is whatever we want it to be" ("Fireworks"). Though delusions are desirable in comedy, they make for misery in *real* life. Ignorance is *not* bliss. Put that in your GE appliance and microwave it.

NOTES

1. For a more detailed discussion of this idea, check out Adam Barkman, "Negative Happiness," *Kritike: An Online Journal of Philosophy* 3, no. 1 (June 2009): 72–77. www .kritike.org/journal/issue_5/barkman_june2009.pdf.

2. Plato, *The Republic* (Oxford: Oxford University Press, 1995), 514a–518b.

3. Ibid.

4. John 14:6.

OF COOKIE JARS AND CEOs: TIME AND SELF ON *30 ROCK*

Tyler Shores

How do we relate to the past? What does the past mean to us? To what extent can we hope to understand the role that the past plays in our present everyday lives? Questions such as these occur over and over again for the characters of *30 Rock*. For example, when Jack Donaghy hires a private investigator to snoop into his own past for anything that might compromise his chances at the CEO position, we discover an unexpected hobby.

> Lenny: You don't have a massive collection of cookie jars, do you?
>
> Jack: How did you find out about that?
>
> Lenny: This is bad. CEOs don't have thousands of cookie jars. Weird little guys in bow ties do. You hear what I'm getting at?
>
> Jack: What? Are you saying it's a gay thing?

Lenny: You wish it was a gay thing. This is worse—you've gotta get rid of them!

The cookie jar collection represents an attachment to the past for Jack that he isn't quite ready to sever, however willing (or unwilling) he might be to acknowledge how personally important that part of the past is to him.

Liz: What's with the cookie jar?

Jack: I collect them.

Liz: Really? Is that some sort of unresolved childhood thing?

Jack: Nice try. Uh, we never had any cookie jars in my home because my mother never baked us any cookies because she never felt we deserved any cookies. So obviously it has nothing to do with my childhood.

Liz: But that cookie jar says "MOM" on it.

Jack: Uh, I don't think so. I've always viewed it as an upside-down "WOW."

In order to secure his hopes at future happiness in the form of that CEO promotion, Jack is forced to make a choice between the past and the future, as his private investigator advises him: "You can either be head of the largest corporation in America, or get buried in a bow tie with a bunch of cookie jars" ("The Collection"). In the end, Jack can't bring himself to destroy the cookie jars, and finds a new home for his collection with Kenneth, who happens to be a like-minded cookie jar enthusiast.[1]

In whatever form such encounters with the past take—whether it's unresolved family issues (Jack's relationship with his mother, his estranged con artist brother, and long-lost biological father); unfulfilled childhood dreams (Tracy had always dreamt of being an astronaut, Pete wanted to be a congressman);

or even old favorite television shows (Kenneth and his wish for a final episode of *Night Court*)—the characters on *30 Rock* find themselves returning again and again to their past.

Moments of past meeting present become instances of encountering past selves: who we once were, and who we are now. In this chapter, we'll look at what the past means to the present, what the present means to the past, and how these cumulative encounters with the past might lead to a better understanding of how we come to be the self that we are now, and the self that we may yet become in the future.

Theory of Self: Who Are We?

Questions of the self and personal identity are in many ways central to all of our other questions. Our understanding of what the self means is our window to the rest of the world and shapes the way we relate to and understand everything around us. At the same time, we are inherently temporal beings: our sense of self is bound closely to the way in which we relate to time. We understand our existence in terms of a past, a present, and a future.

The question of who we are from one period of time to the next (or even from moment to moment) has important ethical implications. For example, when Liz has to undertake compulsory sexual harassment training—or, as Jack calls them, "pervert seminars" ("Jackie Jormp Jomp")—certain assumptions are made about the self over time. The assumption is that the Liz Lemon of the current moment who is undergoing the training is the same Liz Lemon who committed the offense in the past, followed by the further assumption that the present training will prevent Liz Lemon's future self from committing future acts of sexual harassment.[2]

The philosopher Alfred North Whitehead (1861–1947) offers another way of thinking about this question of the self over time. We might think of the self as who a person is in a single moment, or over a series of moments in time, or perhaps a defining characteristic of "self-ness" that extends throughout time. As he says:

> There are three different ways of thinking of a person. The most concrete way is to identify the person with a single occasion of experience. . . . To speak of the person in this way is to speak of the self-at-one-moment. The second way to speak of a person is as a historical thread of occasions over time. The third way of thinking of a person would be to speak of a defining characteristic through a series of occasions. The first suggests a theory of a person at any given time. The latter suggest personal identity over time. The one, however, is not separable from the other.[3]

Fundamental to Whitehead's thinking is a certain continuity of the self. But another philosopher, David Hume (1711–1776), is skeptical that we can be the same person from even five minutes ago, let alone over the course of a lifetime:

> There are some philosophers, who imagine we are every moment intimately conscious of what we call our SELF; that we feel its existence and its continuance in existence. . . . For my part, when I enter most intimately into what I call *myself*, I always stumble on some particular perception or other, of heat or cold, light or shade, love or hatred, pain or pleasure. I never can catch *myself* at any time without a perception, and never can observe anything but the perception.[4]

Hume's conception is of a discontinuous self, in which we are best described as "a bundle or collection of different perceptions which succeed one another with an inconceivable rapidity and are in perpetual flux and movement."[5] We are who we are now, but nothing can empirically guarantee we know who we are compared to who we were or will be. If we consider

Hume's view of the self as being dependent upon what we are conscious of at a given moment, then time becomes condensed into "a series of nows"[6] and our sense of self feels oddly reduced. Whether we accept or reject Hume's proposition, we might still acknowledge that we are never *exactly* the same person that we were, by virtue of the fact that we're always experiencing new thoughts and impressions that cumulatively shape a newer sense of self.

Augustine (354–430) questions the complex relationship between past, present, and future in human consciousness by considering whether we should assume that there are "three times—a present of the past, a present of the present, and a present of the future." Instead, Augustine suggests that these three time states "exist in the mind, and I do not see them anywhere else: the present time of things past is memory; the present time of things present is sight; the present time of things future is expectation."[7] As we shall see, this consideration of time in terms of mental experience is an important key to Jack Donaghy's complicated relationship with his past.

Apollo, Apollo: Jack Donaghy and Our Encounter with the Past

On his fiftieth birthday, Jack watches home movies of his tenth birthday party. His ten-year-old self receives a gift (we can't see what's in the box) that makes him so excited that he throws up. (Jack's throwing up is akin to what Lemon calls "lizzing.")[8] The memory prompts Jack to wonder about that younger self from a happier, simpler time in relation to the person he is today.

> Jack: I wonder what that ten-year-old would think if he could see himself now . . .
>
> Liz: Well, if that kid could see himself today . . . he would throw up. ["Apollo, Apollo"]

Jack's reflection on that ten-year-old version of himself raises important questions: is Jack the same person that he was forty years ago? To what extent can we define the relationship between our past selves and our present selves? Our encounters with the past, whether we realize it or not, create a sort of inner tension within our consciousness—a split between our awareness of who we are now and who we once were. Notice for instance that when Jack looks at his younger self, he doesn't say "myself" but instead "that ten year old." We both identify with and differentiate ourselves from our past self; we can't be both our past self and present self at the same time.

The philosopher Gilbert Ryle (1900–1976) discusses this seeming split between our present consciousness and consciousness of the past (what he calls "the elusiveness of 'I'") by suggesting that when thinking about ourselves, we are always already lagging behind, because our thought is always relegated to the past as soon as the moment of conceiving that thought has passed. Ryle says that our sense of self in this way is always our shadow, which we can both never catch, yet never escape from—someone who attempts to separate those past and present moments of consciousness therefore "never succeeds in jumping on to the shadow of his own head, yet he is never more than one jump behind."[9] We are left with two different selves in time, past and present, which can never quite meet. In other words, perhaps we are limited by the scope of our consciousness, because the "present continuously becomes past, and by the time we take stock of it we are in another present, consumed with planning the future . . . the present is never here. We are hopelessly late for consciousness."[10]

In this same episode, Jack looks back upon a list he made in the fifth grade of things he wanted to have done by the time he was fifty years old ("go to Disneyland; ride in an airplane; kiss Peggy Fleming; live in a house with stairs; beat up a Russian; hit Mom with a car"). Jack has managed with an impressive degree of fidelity to follow his ten-year-old self's life goals—the only thing left on his list is "be friends with Batman," which Jack promptly decides to do by inviting Adam West to his birthday party that evening. Yet in the aftermath of that birthday party, Jack finds himself waxing nostalgic in a Citizen Kane–esque moment while again watching that old home movie from his tenth birthday.

> Jack: What's inside that box? What happens to us? I have a good life, but I'll never be that happy again. I want that back.

> Liz: Well, there's nothing you can do about that.

> Jack: I disagree. I'm going to find out what was inside that box. I'm going to buy it with money and it is going to make me happy. If that doesn't work I'm going to Benjamin Button myself.

Is Jack's definition of a good life simply being able to list a number of accomplishments from his past? The question of what our past selves think would make our future selves happy is worth considering. Jean-Jacques Rousseau (1712–1778) addresses just how difficult it can be to find that elusive goal of happiness when we take into account our selves as temporal beings:

> Always out ahead of us or lagging behind, they recall a past which is gone or anticipate a future which may never come into being; there is nothing solid there for the heart to attach itself to. . . . how can we give the name of happiness to a fleeting state which leaves our hearts empty and anxious, either regretting something that is past or desiring something that is yet to come?[11]

Jack goes on a quest to find whatever is in that box, whatever it was that once made him so happy that he vomited. The search for what was in that box is even more a search for a past self and past happiness than it is for the thing that Jack finds: an Apollo Lunar Module toy. Yet, after finding the object of his past happiness, Jack reluctantly realizes, "That part of me is gone forever. I guess I just see the world the way I see it."

Was Hume right? Can we only hope to be the person that we are in the present, and are we left to doubt whether any continuity of who we are is recoverable from our past to our present, and our future? "The person, whom we take to have a continuing identity, seems upon closer analysis to have a past that is no more, a future that is not yet, and a present that will not endure. So what is the continuing self?"[12] But the episode does not end on quite that note. Jack does rediscover some of that long-buried happiness, although not in the place that he expected to find it. While the writers are having a good laugh watching Liz's one acting job (a commercial for "a chatline for urban singles," according to Liz), Jack laughs so hard that he vomits for the first time in forty years. And afterward he says, "I feel great, I feel like a kid" ("Apollo, Apollo"). It wasn't the object from the past in the form of that Apollo Lunar Module that was any different, but Jack himself was different; his perspective toward the past had changed. Yet:

> for all the changes . . . he discovered, through memory, a continuity in his life that . . . made him the same person in his youth as in his maturity (and old age); that though the past was past and therefore did not exist, it nevertheless, through memory, had its own, peculiarly potent kind of reality in the present—the presence of things past.[13]

Though Jack is not exactly the same person that he was forty years ago, there is still some part of him that can find the happiness he was afraid he had lost.

Liz Lemon and High School: The More Things Change, the More They Don't

Whereas Jack's encounter with the past was an attempt to recover a past self, Liz's encounter with her own past experiences becomes an attempt to differentiate herself from that past. While contemplating whether to go to her high school reunion, Liz is more than a little hesitant, because she was, in her own words, "kind of a lonely nerd in high school." Jack, however, convinces her to confront that past by emphasizing who she is now, not who she was then:

> Liz: The only people that are going to go to this thing are . . . the cool, pretty crowd.
>
> Jack: Well, that's you now, Lemon. You run a hit TV show. You have very impressive friends. You found a hairstyle that works for you so long as it's not too humid. And you're telling me you don't have the confidence to face a bunch of whittling, jug blowing, IHOP monkeys?
>
> Liz: Jack, it's a suburb of Philadelphia.

At the high school reunion, contrary to her memories of herself as the lonely nerd, Liz is shocked to discover that she actually made life a living hell for everyone around her, and was universally feared and hated. While discovering that she was not the person that she had thought or remembered herself being, Liz attempts on the spot to become a "new Liz," a nicer Liz to atone for her past meanness.

But it quickly becomes apparent just how interconnected the past and present are; Liz's attempts to hold the past and the present apart do not go terribly well. In fact, she seems to be causing just as much harm in her efforts to be nicer. Fed up with being New Liz, she quickly reverts to Old Liz:

> Liz: If these jagweeds don't want to get to know the nice, new me, then screw them and their rapidly yellowing teeth!
>
> Jack: Wow, Lemon: you really haven't changed have you?

Liz: Excuse me?

Jack: What happened when I told you Geiss had screwed me over for the CEO job? Did you offer your help as a friend? Or did you make some joke about me being impotent?

Liz: Jeez, that was like eight hours ago! ["Reunion"]

Liz's response is telling. How much can we change, whether over the course of many years, or half a day? Where does our past self leave off and our present self begin? Apparently for Liz, she can find some of the continuity of self that both Augustine and Whitehead advocate, for better or for worse.

We can't help but believe in a certain continuity of self and individual experience over time. Like Jack and his ten-year-old self, we want to believe to some extent that the past is recoverable, and therefore our past selves are as well. Just as we reach backward in time to ponder our past selves, we look forward into the future to speculate about the person that we might become. But encounters with possible future selves can be far from pleasant. When Liz visits her comedy writing idol, Rosemary Howard[14], a figure who represents a connecting point between her past (who she hoped to become someday) and her future (who she then fears she might become after her demystifying encounter), she is forced to realize: "It was terrible. I went to her apartment. I don't think she has a toilet! I saw my future, Jack" ("Rosemary's Baby"). From Liz's experience we see clearly that what we thought our past self wanted in the future is not always what our present self actually wants when that future becomes our present.

One way of thinking about this relationship between our past, present, and future selves is that we are constantly reinterpreting and reevaluating what the past means to us in the present. As with Jack's Apollo Lunar Module, we are constantly endowing the past with different meaning based on the person we are in the present moment. What the past means necessarily evolves with our developing sense of self. That experience of knowing now what we didn't know then is akin to Sigmund Freud's (1856–1939) concept of *Nachtraglichkeit*, or "afterwardsness"[15]—the idea is that in looking retrospectively upon the past, we cannot help but project what we already know in our current state onto that past. Our memories of the past therefore provide us with some continuity between the person we were, and the person we are—although, as we've seen from Liz's own memories of high school, our memory is far from a guarantee of an accurate recollection of the way things actually were. For Augustine, who wrote expansively on the topic of memory in his *Confessions*, memory represents a means of continuity of the self from past, to present, and into future. In memory, says Augustine:

> I encounter myself; I recall myself—what I have done, when and where I did it, and in what state of mind I was at the time. . . . I can make myself weave them into the context of the past, and from them I can infer future actions, events, hopes, and then I can contemplate all these as though they were in the present.[16]

We make sense of the past and present by placing them within a meaningful context that is mutually defining—just as our encounters with the past may affect our present experience, the perspective of our present selves changes the way in which we relate to our past.

What the past means to us is altered over time, as is our sense of self. Concerned as we are with looking backward into the past and forward into the future, "only the present is actual. The past is *no longer now*, and therefore *no longer actual*. The future is *yet to be now*, and therefore *yet to be actual*."[17] Much like Jack and his cookie jars, we are often confronted with choices between who we were, and who we are. Do we always make the right choices? Let's look at Jenna, for example:

> Liz: You can try to fight getting older. You can be like Madonna and cling to youth with your Gollum arms. Or you can be like Meryl Streep and embrace your age with elegance.
>
> Jenna: So you're saying it's a choice? Between the dignity of middle age and the illusion of youth.
>
> Liz: Two paths—Meryl Streep . . . or Madonna.
>
> Jenna: Very well. I will emulate my acting inspiration. A woman of profound poise, whose career is what we all aspire to—
>
> Liz: Okay, this buildup is making me nervous.
>
> Jenna: —a woman whose feminine grace and normal outfits are an inspiration—
>
> Liz: Just say who it is, and I'll feel better.
>
> Jenna: —someone whose very name stands for enduring beauty and the wonder of womanhood!
>
> Liz: Please don't say—
>
> Jenna: Madonna! ["Black Light Attack!"]

Hopefully, unlike Jenna in this instance, we sometimes make the right decisions. We understand that the past is part of who we are. We are temporal beings, yet we find it difficult or impossible to neatly differentiate where our past, present, and future begin and end.

NOTES

1. It's too bad this isn't a chapter on psychoanalysis, because we might find the following exchange about cookie jars between Jack and Kenneth especially interesting:

> Kenneth: Huh! Look at the old kooky old cookie jar! I like the upside down "WOW" on it!

Jack: You like cookie jars, Kenneth.

Kenneth: I guess I never thought about it that much. We had a nice one back home in Georgia. Had a bear on it. I remember when my mom's friend Ron would come over. They'd go into the bedroom to sort out their paperwork. And, I'd just go ahead and stare at that cookie jar. It was almost as if I took every problem that I ever had and I put it inside that cookie jar. And I sealed it up so tight that nothing would ever, ever, ever get out. So, I guess to answer your question, I'd give cookie jars about a "B"!

Jack: Some people have so many problems, there's not enough cookie jars in the world to contain them.

Kenneth: Well, that just makes me sad.

2. Immediately after completing her training, Liz makes a pass at the HR person, Jeffrey Weinerslave, in order to get resuspended from work.

3. Alfred North Whitehead, *Symbolism: Its Meaning and Effect* (New York: Fordham University Press, 1995), 27–28.

4. David Hume, *A Treatise of Human Nature*, edited by David Fate Norton and Mary J. Norton (Oxford: Oxford University Press, 2000), 164–165.

5. Hume, *A Treatise of Human Nature*, 165.

6. Edmund Husserl, *On the Phenomenology of the Consciousness of Internal Time*, translated by John Barnett Brough (Dordrecht: Kluwer Academic Publishers 1991), 181.

7. Saint Augustine, *Confessions*, translated by Rex Warner (New York: New American Library, 1963), 268.

8. Which, according to Liz, is a combination of laughing and whizzing, for those of us who really wanted to know.

9. Gilbert Ryle, *The Concept of Mind* (London: Penguin Books, 2000), 187.

10. Antonio Damasio, *Descartes' Error* (New York: Harper, 1995), 240.

11. Jean-Jacques Rousseau, *Reveries of the Solitary Walke*, translated by Peter France (Penguin Books: New York, 1979), 88.

12. Olav Bryant Smith, *Myths of the Self: Narrative Identity and Postmodern Metaphysics* (Lanham, MD: Lexington Books, 2004), 152.

13. James Olney, *Memory & Narrative: The Weave of Life-Writing* (Chicago: University of Chicago Press, 1998), 38.

14. Of course, Rosemary has her own issues with temporality to deal with:

Liz: Have you been drinking wine all day?

Rosemary: Oh, it's heart healthy.

Liz: All day?!

Rosemary: Oh come on, Liz! It's the nineties!

15. Nicola King, *Memory, Narrative, Identity: Remembering the Self* (Edinburgh: Edinburgh University Press, 2000), 11.

16. Saint Augustine, *Confessions*, 211.

17. Bryant Smith, *Myths of the Self*, 75.

ONE CITY'S CHEESE-CURL ADDICT IS ANOTHER CITY'S MODEL: A QUESTION OF TASTE

Michael Da Silva and Melina Found

After a routine walk down the street results in both a police search and a New Yorker spitting in Lemon's mouth, Liz decides she needs a vacation. Soon she's off to Cleveland with her boyfriend Floyd. Things are different there. In Cleveland, the police do not search Lemon; instead they ask her if she wants to pet a police horse. No one spits in Lemon's mouth, and everyone she passes on the street says hello. As Lemon walks through a park, a woman stops to ask, "Are you a model?" When Lemon answers in the negative, the woman responds, "You are so skinny. You really should eat something." Given Lemon's love of cheese curls and ignorance of the exercise equipment in her New York apartment, this perspective on her body image is a pleasant surprise. The emphasis on her good looks continues when Lemon is offered a job as the host of a cooking show on WKYZ. In Cleveland, Lemon belongs on TV rather than behind the scenes. Indeed, the trip proves so inspiring that Lemon considers moving to Cleveland with Floyd, who is a native.

Lemon leaves town with two problems remaining in New York: one, Jack Donaghy's controversial romance with Phoebe; and two, Tracy Jordan's feud with the Black Crusaders, a group of elite African Americans like Bill Cosby, Oprah Winfrey, and Phoebe from *Sesame Street* who consider Tracy a walking stereotype and an "embarrassment to African Americans." These problems don't disappear while Lemon is on vacation. Rather than tackling the issues head-on as she does in most episodes, Lemon is aggravated by these problems. New York seems unnecessarily complicated compared to Cleveland. Lemon looks forward to moving to Cleveland and avoiding these problems, and tells Jack as much. Jack, in turn, tells Lemon that she will not move:

> Jack: Every great romantic getaway has that moment where you want to pack it up and stay. That's how I ended up with a time share in Port Arthur, Texas.

> Liz: We don't think that's what this is. I mean Floyd is great and, look, I'm a model in Cleveland.

> [*Liz shows Jack a flyer with Liz modeling clothing on the front page.*]

> Jenna Maroney: Yeah, we're all models west of the Allegheny.

It's tempting to interpret this exchange (and indeed the whole episode "Cleveland") as an example of how the grass is always greener on the other side. Donaghy suggests this in his assessment of the situation. As a descriptive fact of Lemon's experience in Cleveland, it's true—but it's not philosophically interesting. By contrast, Lemon's experience of being model caliber in Cleveland and Maroney's claim that it is to be expected pose some interesting philosophical questions.

Are all women "models west of the Alleghany," or only all New Yorkers? The latter seems more likely, but one philosophically interesting thing is clear in either case: different places have different aesthetic values. One city's cheese curl addict is another city's model.

It Takes Two to Go Back to the 1980s: A Brief Introduction to Social Constructivism

30 Rock is a great source of nostalgia. Guest stars like the 1970s and 1980s *Star Wars* actor and sex symbol Carrie Fisher are rescued from obscurity to play prominent roles in the series. Likewise, hit songs from that era are frequently invoked. In "Mamma Mia" for example, Liz Lemon and Pete Hornberger try to gauge Tracy Jordan's age by singing a song that everyone from Liz and Pete's generation is supposed to know, namely "It Takes Two" by Rob Base and DJ E-Z Rock. When Tracy is unable to sing the chorus of the song and instead sings a jazz standard, Liz and Pete determine that Tracy must be older than he looks. Popular culture references are an essential part of the *30 Rock* experience. Many of these references are to popular culture artifacts from the era of the creator and star Tina Fey's coming-of-age, the 1980s. Fey is able to reappropriate these artifacts for nostalgic purposes, while simultaneously repopularizing them in a new context. In keeping with this spirit of nostalgia, let's turn back to the 1990s.

The 1990s were the era of the so-called Culture Wars between scientists and professors in the humanities and social sciences. The issue at the center of the "Wars" was whether there are scientific facts of nature or if scientific knowledge is simply a product of cultural practices. Most scientists were on the side of scientific facts, a seemingly necessary prerequisite for scientific practice. The physicist Alan Sokal famously exposed the pretensions of so-called theorists by publishing "Transgressing the Boundaries: Towards a Transformative Hermeneutics of Quantum Gravity," a parody of cultural theory in one of the leading cultural theory journals, *Social Text*.

According to the philosopher Ian Hacking, the Culture Wars "can be focused on social construction."[1] The combatants can be more clearly divided between proponents and opponents of social construction than they can between working scientists and academics, although most working scientists do oppose social construction, and social construction's advocates are predominantly sociologists. It is, however, difficult to say what exactly social construction is. Hacking asserts that "social constructivists about X tend to hold that . . . X need not have existed, or need not be at all. X, or X as it is at present, is not determined by the nature of things; it is not inevitable."[2] Any given scientific fact, on this view, is not determined by nature, but is a social construct. In a different social setting, its opposite could be affirmed. Likewise, Lemon the neurotic, out-of-shape New Yorker could be otherwise. And she is—in Cleveland!

Liz the model is a creation of Cleveland. Even human beings seem to be capable of social construction. She needn't be the way she is. The notion that even we can be socially constructed is not new. Hacking offers numerous examples of individuals who hold this view, from a Catholic social worker to the prominent philosopher Sally Haslanger. Hacking, however, believes that even these thinkers are "unenterprising . . . [in their view that] we are the way we are, to some substantial extent, because of what is attributed to us, and what we attribute to ourselves."[3] It's obvious that Liz Lemon is a model because others attribute a model's characteristics to her. She is told she looks like a model, and then actually becomes one.

It's unclear just how enterprising one can be in one's social construction before becoming a true combatant in the Culture Wars. Part of the problem is that no one seems to know exactly what social constructivists believe is being constructed.

Hacking's book *The Social Construction of What?* points to this problem. What gets socially constructed? Is it stuff, or is it theories about stuff? Is the subject of the debate ontological (dealing with the reality of things), epistemological (dealing with knowledge), or something else?

Social constructions of a wide variety of topics have been proposed from authorship to Zulu nationalism.[4] Here we'll avoid the numerous problems with strictly defining social constructivism and its aims. Instead, we'll turn to one form of the social construction of aesthetic experience in order to examine whether values could be socially constructed. After all, it's the very perception of Liz Lemon that appears to be socially constructed both in Cleveland and in "Cleveland."

"How *Sex and the City* Are We Right Now? I'm Samantha, You're Charlotte, and You're the Lady at Home Who Watches It.": Why Lemon Does Not Fit with the Aesthetics of New York

Social constructivism has been applied in value-related fields, like aesthetics. For example, in "The Social Construction of Aesthetic Response," the philosopher Marcia Muelder Eaton explores the possibility that our aesthetic judgments may be formed by our social setting and thus are context-dependent. Lemon is comfortable in her "work sneakers" and clothes that Donaghy doubts were purchased from a women's store. Meanwhile, she is judged by the aesthetic views of a New York population that expects everyone to wear Prada shoes, Dolce and Gabbana sunglasses, and clothes straight off that season's runway.

To explain the theory that one's aesthetic sense is formed by one's context or culture, Eaton suggests it results in part from "what communities consider worth drawing attention to."[5] Aesthetic response involves reacting to what the community regards as important in the manner that community prescribes. Eaton thus advocates the view that aesthetic responses are at least partially socially constructed.

Focusing on the theory that aesthetic response is socially constructed, Eaton highlights three arguments that support the idea: that it is learned; that it is culture-bound; and that it is socially prescribed and proscribed. In examining the view that aesthetic response is learned, Eaton suggests it develops from the learned "capacity to judge and compare."[6] Being able to tell that Cerie Xerox does not really need to wear a bra and that Lemon's stained shirts are unsightly comes from learning to contrast their appearances. A well-trained eye would be able to notice the expensive cut of Donaghy's suit and Lemon's paltry, department store track pants. Furthermore, different demographics have differing aesthetic senses and roles. Lemon's middle-class status places her in a different aesthetic category than Donaghy or Maroney, who both comfortably fall into the role of critic. Consider Donaghy's appraisal of Lemon's outfit in the series pilot:

> Lemon: But I'm not dressed for that.
>
> Donaghy: You are dressed for Burger King. Should we make it Burger King?

By way of an extensive education and experience in the business world, Donaghy has developed what is commonly called "taste." Taste, in turn, is constituted by educational practices and business norms. Part of taste is knowing what to wear in a given situation. Lemon seems to have the requisite background to know what *not* to wear in a situation. Lacking Donaghy's background, however, Lemon doesn't know much more than that. In the pilot, Lemon's idea of business attire seems better suited to Burger King than it does to the workplace. Lemon's middle-class background results in middle-class taste.

Eaton's idea that aesthetic response is culture-bound suggests it is a response to "intrinsic properties that a culture values."[7] In the context of New York, where fashion, the arts, and the A-list are revered, Maroney's comment becomes understandable, as she views the world "west of the Allegheny" with aesthetic values honed in the Big Apple. To fully appreciate a culture's aesthetic values, we have to be aware of its history. Artists like Andy Warhol and Jackson Pollock helped to establish New York as the international visual arts capital. Warhol's pop art in particular focused on the idea of celebrity and the culture of fascination with Hollywood icons. In the fashion world, designers such as Donna Karan and Marc Jacobs have made New York their headquarters and have added to its rise as one of the top five fashion hubs of the world. There's little chance for Lemon to compete with haute couture models.

The question is now whether the aesthetic views of Maroney, Donaghy, and the differing views of Lemon are justified. On *30 Rock*, the justification comes primarily from class standing. It's worth remembering, however, that the upper class is often composed of former middle-class individuals. While Lemon has yet to develop taste, she can potentially acquire taste as she climbs the ladder of success as Donaghy's protégé. This is hinted at by her ability to get faux-millionaire Gavin Valure to watch MTV Canada. When the middle class becomes part of the upper class, it changes the social dynamic and, in turn, the aesthetic judgments of the class or city.

Lemon often tries, but she hasn't succeeded in acquiring or transforming taste yet. We learn about her failed attempt at wearing shorts to work; watch Jack Donaghy discover a pair of Spanx in Lemon's apartment; see her desperately trying to be professional, only to hear, "You've got lettuce in your hair." Disregarding the obvious comedic value of pointing out Liz's flaws, Lemon is an easy aesthetics target by New York standards. The aesthetic standards of New York match the pace of the city, demanding and rigorous. The cutting edge of aesthetics is always in flux, and to miss one minute means to be judged the next minute. Cleveland may be the birthplace of Chef Boyardee (as the theme song points out), but it's a long way from Broadway. It may be a more accommodating city, but it is also a slower-paced city. Aesthetic trends thus don't move as quickly, and Lemon can remain on the cutting edge with clothes suitable for a New York Burger King.

Should We Not All Be Able to Agree That Gold Boots Are Ugly?

The success of Tracy Jordan and *TGS with Tracy Jordan* depends on the mantra "You can't question taste." Jordan, the celebrity train wreck and star of such films as *Fat Bitch*, is a master of the low-brow, but it is Jordan who saves *The Girlie Show* from cancellation in *30 Rock*'s pilot episode. If shows were canceled on the basis of quality alone or, alternatively, every *TGS* fan could be so routinely chastised for watching low-brow television that every fan would stop watching the show, then Jordan's particular brand of humor couldn't succeed. Even the phrase "low-brow," however, denotes a hierarchy of values. It suggests a difference in quality between the award-winning *30 Rock* and the show within it, *TGS with Tracy Jordan*. Even as we affirm low-brow humor, we suggest it is of lesser quality by using the evaluative term "low-brow." The idea that "you can't question taste" seems to suggest that all aesthetic judgments are equally valuable. Everyone is free to say one show is better than another, but paradoxically, these contradictory claims are equally valuable. This is a form of relativism, and social constructivism's critics suggest that it is one reason to fear social constructivism.

The idea that any aesthetic judgment is equally valuable can seem terrifying, not only when you consider Liz Lemon's many comic foibles, but also when you consider some of Tracy Jordan's more extravagant clothing decisions. In one episode, for instance, Jordan fears that if he doesn't spend all his money, his wife will divorce him in order to take half his fortune. Jordan thus buys a pair of solid gold boots. They're so heavy that Jordan cannot lift them off the ground to walk. The humor lies in the fact that solid gold boots are impractical. Fashion critics, however, may also suggest that the gold boots have another fault: like many of Jordan's pieces of bling, the gold boots are extremely gaudy. If all opinions are equally valuable, then fashion critics are free to make this claim, but there is no expert opinion on the value of gold boots, and Jordan remains perfectly capable of asserting that they're the highest form of fashion. Granted, even Jordan realizes that the gold boots are pretty awful, but there's a reason we laugh at his exploits. Jordan's wealth comes in tandem with a lack of taste. Jordan may be Donaghy's rival in pure dollar terms, but Jordan lacks the education and social conditions necessary to develop taste. If there's no real good or bad taste, however, a lot of what makes Jordan funny for *30 Rock* viewers may not exist.

There's a further fear to explore regarding the link between Jordan's wealth and his taste. Jordan's ability to buy the boots stems from his excessive wealth, which also allows him to make a wide range of assertions without facing contradiction. For instance, no one seems to criticize his proposed Thomas Jefferson film "with all the claymation sex scenes." His proposed Michael McDonald cover album is also considered a viable part of a comeback. One fear of aesthetic relativism is that where there's no external standard of what's valuable, whoever is in a position of privilege will create the new standard. All opinions may be formally equal in the land of relativism, but certain individuals wield power and influence that others don't. This creates an imbalance of power many wouldn't endorse. Indeed, Hacking points out that many feminist philosophers, such as Lorraine Code, believe that relativism "seems to leave no ground for criticizing oppressive ideas."[8] Oppressive ideas can face no real opposition where the oppressive idea and its counterpart are of equal formal value. Substantively, the oppressive ideas are even further strengthened by the socio- logical fact that those in power often have a better ability to propagate their ideas. Where all ideas are equal, the rulers' ideas are binding because they are the rulers' ideas and there are no reasonable grounds to oppose them. Consider the fact that Jordan's proposed McDonald cover album is only canceled due to the whims of a higher authority, the Black Crusaders, who find Jordan's work to be in poor taste. Here, the Black Crusaders' power gives them the authority to impose their taste on others.

Where aesthetic judgment is a sociological phenomenon, it's worth remembering the fact that celebrities wield great judgment over what is considered fashionable in many Western societies. Their exposure allows them to spread new ideas. Jerry Seinfeld's promotion of *Bee Movie* in "SeinfeldVision" is an example of this. He's able to assert his opinion that his film is worth watching on a wide platform, a Thursday night NBC sitcom. There are no real experts in a relativistic world, so Seinfeld's perspective is of equal formal value with any critical perspective, but Seinfeld has the added edge of a wider audience. The more people that hear his opinion, the more people who are willing to endorse it. If aesthetic judgment was simply a matter of opinion and Jordan wore his gold boots on television, there would be no external standard by which one could judge their value. Only intuition, common sense, and personal criteria for aesthetic judgment could prevent individuals from buying their own gold boots. A widespread phenomenon of gold-boots-wearing could follow, and getting around would suddenly be a lot more difficult!

Granted, many people wouldn't be able to afford these boots, but the general point still stands. If society is the creator and barometer of value, then there's no external standard for judging opinions. This is a form of relativism. If values are socially constructed, then one major source of that construction is celebrity endorsement. Surely there must be some way for critics of gold boots to provide rational arguments to oppose their propagation, but the lack of an external standard silences the critical voice. While our example here is a silly one, Code points to more serious, political reasons why this could be problematic. Nevertheless, it's possible to be a social constructivist without being a relativist. The philosopher John Searle, for example, has provided an account of social facts that avoids any kind of relativism.[9] We will simply point out how a relativistic social constructivism could be problematic. We will not stand idly by as our friends and neighbors choose to wear gold boots!

You Can Take the Man out of Cleveland . . .

At the end of "Cleveland," Lemon stays in New York while her boyfriend moves back to Cleveland. Perhaps this is for the best. As Floyd points out, "If the whole world moved to their favorite vacation spots, then the whole world would live in Hawaii and Italy and Cleveland." We would hate to see the city ruined by overcrowding. Lemon's staying in New York is also to her benefit, however, because New York defines who she is. In "The Funcooker," for example, Lemon is forced to serve on a jury and misses the hectic set of *TGS with Tracy Jordan*. Her very identity is based on working in the fast-paced setting of a New York City TV show. Indeed, Lemon has become a New Yorker. Even if she hasn't developed its aesthetic values, she's been fundamentally changed by her time in the Big Apple. Floyd, by contrast, grew up in Cleveland and was set in his Cleveland ways even when he moved to New York. He never got used to seeing someone spit in his girlfriend's mouth.

Lemon and Floyd's differing perspectives on New York are the center of their debate on whether they want to settle there permanently. What's clear from this exchange is that what Hacking suggests is an unenterprising form of social constructivism is also a descriptive fact: our social connections and relationships do have an effect on our understanding of our very selves. Changing social settings will change your identity. It will likely also change your aesthetic values. New York Lemon may not be fashionable, but she's far more tasteful than the phone sex worker Chicago Lemon in the episode "Apollo, Apollo." Also clear, however, is that these identities don't change automatically. Floyd remains unchanged by his New York experience. Perhaps this is because Floyd doesn't accept the city as a suitable place to settle. Such an attitude could establish one as an outsider. No one would ascribe a New York identity to an outsider. Regardless of the plausibility of this account of Floyd's New York experience, however, one thing is clear: if society constructs one's self-image and one's values, it does so through a gradual process. In turn, it can take some time for one to change one's social surroundings. This means the gold boot revolution may not come as quickly as we may have suspected earlier, but it also means poor Liz Lemon will have to wait a while until New York accepts her Cleveland-approved cheese curl–loving ways.

NOTES

1. Ian Hacking, *The Social Construction of What?* (Cambridge, MA: Harvard University Press, 1999), 3.

2. Ibid., 6.

3. Ibid., 227.

4. Ibid., 1.

5. Marcia Muelder Eaton, "The Social Construction of Aesthetic Response," *British Journal of Aesthetics*, 35.2 (1995): 95–107, 100.

6. Ibid., 100.

7. Ibid., 102.

8. Hacking, *Social Construction of What?*, 4.

9. John Searle, *The Construction of Social Reality* (New York: Free Press, 1995).

"I'M STRAIGHT-UP MENTALLY ILL": TRACY JORDAN AND TRUE, JUSTIFIED BELIEF

Robert Arp

In an interview with Larry King, Tracy Jordan declares, "New York, as we know it, will no longer exist tomorrow." To be fair, Jordan admits, "Larry, I'm not an expert, but I do have a strong opinion" ("Larry King"). On another occasion Jordan claimed, "I believe the moon doesn't exist. I believe vampires are the world's greatest golfers, but their curse is that they'll never get to prove it. I believe there are thirty-one letters in a white alphabet" ("The Fighting Irish"). Jordan says some pretty crazy stuff, and we all laugh *precisely because* it's so crazy. But Jordan seems to actually *believe* what he says, which makes us laugh even more!

Where does Jordan get such outlandish ideas about vampires and conspiracy theories? What sources or experts does he rely on for the beliefs and "strong opinions" he has? He seems to know a lot of stuff, but it's mostly untrue. So what's the basis for his version of "the truth" or any truths at all? Should anyone have an outlook on the world like Jordan's, where opinions and beliefs seem to be lacking in evidence and justification? These are the kinds of questions that epistemologists explore. Epistemology is the branch of philosophy concerned with the source and nature of knowledge (*episteme* is Greek for "knowledge") as well as with what constitutes the truth, evidence, and justification of our beliefs/opinions.[1] So Jordan is perfect for what we'll be talking about in this chapter because, well, in his own words: "You know the Army be messing with the sun. That's why I keep my junk covered" ("The C Word"). And let's not forget that, according to Jordan, "by burning three different types of meat together, the Tracy Jordan Meat Machine takes bread out of the equation" ("The Rural Juror"). Nuff said.

"Cuz I Don't Believe in One-Way Streets"

In his dialogue *Theaetetus* Plato (428–347 BCE) argued that knowledge consists of (a) a *belief* that is (b) *true* and (c) *justified*. Philosophers ever since have been debating what truth and justification mean.[2] The belief part is pretty easy to understand.

Humans can reason to form beliefs, opinions, and thoughts about themselves, the world, and reality as they perceive it. And of course, Jordan is fond of talking about beliefs and thoughts: "Damn, I can't *believe* we're winning. . . . You got to *think like* these strippers, Liz Lemon. . . . So you *know* I like to minister to transvestite prostitutes . . ." ("SeinfeldVision").

Knowledge includes believing something: to know is, at least, to believe something is the case. So, for example, when Jordan claims about Godzilla, "I know he doesn't care what humans do" ("Secrets and Lies"), he at least *believes*, has the *opinion*, or forms the *thought* that Godzilla does not care what humans do.

"Cuz I Want to Drop Truth Bombs!"

But believing, having an opinion about, or merely forming a thought about something is not enough to know something.

When Jordan claims he knows Godzilla doesn't care what humans do, we don't really think he *knows* that. Why? Because it's just not true. There's no such thing as Godzilla in real life and, even if there were, we probably wouldn't trust Jordan to know what Godzilla thinks anyway. Jordan's full of it; it's just false that he knows this.

So knowledge includes a belief, opinion, or thought about something, but the belief, opinion, or thought also has to be *true*. If what you believe is false, then you don't know it. The people who win on *Jeopardy* know a lot of stuff that is true; the losers don't. When Jordan is talking and role-playing with Jack Donaghy about his (Jordan's) dad, he claims: "All I know is he came from Funky North Philly, he worked in the Campbell Soup factory, and he had a droopy lip due to an untended root canal" ("Rosemary's Baby"). Now, in this case, unlike the Godzilla case, Jordan seems to really know about his dad. Why? Because it's all probably true (true on the show, that is). That's why, along with Donaghy, we actually believe him this time.

When, however, Jordan says, "Do you know it's still illegal to be black in Arizona?" ("Believe in the Stars") we don't think he knows that. At best we think that *he thinks* he knows that it's still illegal to be black in Arizona, but he is obviously confused, again, because it's false. We might say to Jordan, "Sorry, Tracy, you may think, believe, or be of the opinion that it's still illegal to be black in Arizona, but you surely don't know that, because it's false!"

Now, there's a lot of debate about what truth is, or if truth even exists.[3] The most commonsense view of truth is known as the *correspondence theory of truth*. According to this theory, if a belief that someone has actually corresponds or matches up with some state of affairs out there in the world or in reality, then the belief is true. If the belief does not correspond, it's false. This makes sense to most of us who think that there is a distinction between (a) our beliefs about the world or reality and (b) the world or reality as it really is. Notice that we can have beliefs, opinions, or thoughts about the world that are just plain wrong or false, and they're false because they don't correspond with reality.

People on *30 Rock*, like most of us, subscribe to the correspondence theory of truth. When Jordan says something, everyone checks to see if what he says matches up with reality as we know it (or reality on the show). The belief that "vampires are golfers," for example, doesn't correspond with reality, even the reality of the show, so it's obviously false. "I was in Scottie Pippen's wedding" ("Pilot"), claims Jordan. If we could verify this somehow with evidence—say, a picture, a video, someone reliable telling us that this was so—then the claim would be true. Otherwise, Jordan is delusional. To be fair to Tracy, though, Black Crusaders really do seem to exist. So Jordan may have a true belief (on the show) about those people!

"I Know Where That Building Is, I Get My Jamaican Meat Pies There"

Knowledge, as it turns out, is more than just true belief. This is going to sound strange, but it could be the case that you have a true belief about something, yet, you don't *know* that something. You could have a true belief by accident, for example, which is a point that Plato made more than two thousand years ago in the *Theaetetus*. Let's say you thought my first name was Ron, instead of Rob, and someone asked you if you knew my name and what the first letter of my name was. You then said, "Yeah, I know that guy, and I know his name, and it begins with an R." This would be a true belief because my name does begin with an R. But because you thought my name was Ron, instead of Rob, you don't *know* my name, despite having the true belief that my name starts with an R.

More important, when someone claims they know something, we want to know the reason they know that something.

In other words, we want some kind of *justification* for what they claim to know. Remember we said that knowledge consists of (a) a *belief* that is (b) *true* and (c) *justified*. Justification almost always comes in the form of evidence. When Jordan claims he knows where a certain building is, he immediately gives the justification for knowing what he knows. In this case, he presumably has seen the building with his own eyes, because he gets his Jamaican meat pies there, and that is what we take as justification, or evidence, for his knowing where the building is located.

"You Don't Realize How Beautiful a Sunset Is Until It's the Last One You'll Ever See"

Seeing something with one's own eyes is a common form of justification. Consider Jordan's claim here:

> I knew she must have taken those pictures for her boy-friend Sonny cause Sonny used to come over twice a month and you knew when Sonny was coming over because she used to take us to the store and buy two steaks and a bottle of Nair with cocoa butter. ["The Head and the Hair"]

Here, Jordan claims to know things based upon events he has witnessed in the past. As long as these things are true and he has provided us with some justification for his beliefs, we might even say that—believe it or not!—Jordan does know these things.

There are other forms of justification. We can't see everything there is to see with our own eyes. Sometimes we have to rely on a credible source, such as the testimony of another person, to justify what we know. Most of the time, we can rely on what legitimate news sources have to say—not the *National Enquirer* or Creationist pamphlets, of course!—like when the newspaper publishes a picture of Jordan walking out of a

Starbucks in the episode "Jack Meets Dennis." If the newspaper shows a picture of Jordan walking out of a Starbucks and says he was walking out of a Starbucks, then this is justification enough for the rest of us who have not seen it. We can say that we know Jordan was walking out of a Starbucks. Now, of course, newspapers and anyone can be wrong, so we need to always check and double-check our sources, which is something most of us know to do anyway. Tracy claims he was doing The Robot backward into a Starbucks and, if this is true, then the newspaper's report of Jordan walking out of the Starbucks isn't accurate.

Scientists, historians, and geographers can be credible sources of justification as well. As with news sources, however, we need to check and double-check these sources. So when Jordan claims that Martin Luther King said, "I have a feeling," or that he owns property on the Dnieper River in Ukraine, we can check with the historians (and video) to see that MLK actually said, "I have a *dream*," not a feeling ("The Rural Juror"). Jordan is right about the Dnieper River being in Ukraine, according to geographers; but we all bet that it's BS that he owns property there (or, maybe he does?).

You can offer an argument as a form of justification, too. After all, an argument is used to show that a concluding claim you're making is (1) absolutely true (in a deductive argument) and supported by another premise claim, or (2) likely true (in an inductive argument) and supported by another premise claim.[4] Consider this deductive argument that Jordan puts forward as a justification for why he can't be normal:

> I can't be normal. If I'm normal, I'm boring. If I'm boring, I'm not a movie star. If I'm not a movie star, then I'm poor! And poor people can't afford to pay back the $75,000 in cash they owe Quincy Jones! ["Jack Meets Dennis"]

Of course, your argument has to be a good argument in order to be an adequate source of justification. Not only should the conclusion likely follow from the premises (what is called a *strong* inductive argument), or absolutely follow from the premises (what is called a *valid* deductive argument), but all of the premises must, in fact, be true. A strong inductive argument where all of the premises are true is called a *cogent* argument, whereas a valid deductive argument where all of the premises are true is called a *sound* argument. Both cogent and sound arguments are good arguments. I'll let you be the judge of whether Jordan's argument above is sound or not.

"I Could Talk about How the Moon Is a Spy Satellite Put There by Oprah"

There's a famous argument put forward by the philosopher and mathematician W. K. Clifford (1845–1879) in which he concluded that it's "wrong always, everywhere, and for anyone, to believe anything upon insufficient evidence." Clifford used the example of a shipbuilder who allows his ship to be used by people to emigrate, without knowing, for sure, if the ship is seaworthy. The ship turns out not to be seaworthy, the emigrants drown, and the shipbuilder "got his insurance money when she went down in mid-ocean and told no tales." Clifford maintained that the shipbuilder is morally responsible for the deaths of the emigrants. Why? Because the shipbuilder didn't take the time to justify his belief that the ship was seaworthy this time around. Here, we have a moral argument for making damn well sure that we *really do know* what we think we know. In other words, we better always make sure that, at the very least, our beliefs are true and we have solid justification for the truth of our beliefs. According to Clifford: "Every time we let ourselves believe for unworthy reasons, we weaken our powers of self-control, of doubting, of judicially and fairly weighing evidence."[5] This is sound rational advice, and it turns out to be sound moral advice too.

So while we all laugh at Tracy Jordan, in all seriousness, the crazy stuff that comes out of his mouth, if he believes it—and especially, if he wants *others* to believe it—isn't actually a good thing, and it might be downright immoral. Can you imagine what the kids in Jordan's household must think? The moon is a spy satellite put there by Oprah? Vampires exist? Conspiracy theories? "Affirmative action was designed to keep women and minorities in competition with each other. To distract us while white dudes inject AIDS into our chicken nuggets" ("Pilot")? Jeez! Liz Lemon is right: Tracy Jordan really *does* have mental issues. In fact, Tracy Jordan is right: he is straight-up mentally ill!

"Nothing Unusual. Russian Mobs, Invisible Motorcycles, Sex Pooping."

I want to echo the empiricist philosopher, David Hume (1711–1776), who claimed, "A wise man, therefore, proportions his belief to the evidence." This makes sense to us when we stop to think about it; but how often do we really take the time to make sure our beliefs are both true and justified? For years I took it for granted and believed blindly that some kind of god really did exist, that Jesus was that god, and that the Catholic Church was the one and only revealer of that god's wishes. Now, having sought justification for these beliefs, I see that there are a whole host of problems with them that force me to, at the very least, stop taking them for granted. I must confess that these beliefs, for me, are very similar to the belief in invisible motorcycles.

When all is said and done, and as crazy as the real-life Tracy Jordan–types are in this world—with their beliefs that are neither true nor justified—the *30 Rock* Tracy Jordan makes this wise claim: "Our comedy gotta do more than make people laugh. Gotta make people think" ("The Break-Up"). You have succeeded, Tracy!

NOTES

1. Good introduction to epistemology texts include: Robert Audi, *Epistemology: A Contemporary Introduction* (London: Routledge, 2003); and Jack Crumley, *Introduction to Epistemology* (Columbus, OH: McGraw-Hill, 1998).

2. See Plato's *Theaetetus*, in *Plato: Complete Works*, edited by John M. Cooper (Indianapolis, IN: Hackett Publishing Company, 1997).

3. Good places to start thinking about truth include the sections on truth in: Audi, *Epistemology* and Crumley, *Introduction to Epistemology*.

4. For more on arguments and critical thinking in general, see Gregory Bassham, William Irwin, Henry Nardone, and James M. Wallace, *Critical Thinking: A Student's Introduction* (New York: McGraw-Hill, 2004); Robert Arp, "The Chewbacca Defense: A *South Park* Logic Lesson," in *South Park and Philosophy: You Know, I Learned Something Today*, edited by Robert Arp (Malden, MA: Blackwell Publishers, 2007), 40–54.

5. See W. K. Clifford, *The Ethics of Belief and Other Essays*, edited by Timothy Madigan (Amherst, NY: Prometheus Books, 1999).

PERFORMING AT *30 ROCK* (AND EVERYWHERE ELSE)

Marc E. Shaw

Playing at *30 Rock*

Shakespeare famously wrote, "All the world's a stage, and all the men and women merely players." That you and I are performers in our daily lives remains a familiar idea. The repertoire that you perform each day includes your social roles at work and the repeated daily actions of your identity: gender, age, race, and more. On *30 Rock*, the performance of self provides fertile ground for what this sitcom does best: staging outrageous characters and satirically insightful moments at 30 Rockefeller Center. *30 Rock* isn't *The Cosby Show* or *Everybody Loves Raymond*, where a central family keeps matters close to home. Instead, as in *The Office* or *Mad Men*, the vocational location is everything. 30 Rockefeller Center itself becomes the stage where all play their roles in both a theatrical and corporate sense: Liz Lemon, the industrious head writer; Jack Donaghy, the demanding executive; Kenneth, the trusty page; and Jenna and Tracy, the flaky but ultimately loyal lead actors.

Philosophers are wary of performance in the social realm, especially the workplace. Plato (ca. 428–348 BCE) was suspicious of any sort of role imitation, believing that mimetic, or imitative, actions are simply too far removed from reality to do anyone any good. If you're busy copying some other character—simply *playing at* being something—you'll likely make more mistakes about what's real and what isn't. You're more likely to come to bizarre views when you don't concentrate on *reality*, and instead occupy your time with mere imitation. Just consider Tracy Jordan to appreciate Plato's worry.

The German philosopher Friedrich Nietzsche (1844–1900) warns, "If someone wants to *seem* to be something, stubbornly and for a long time, he eventually finds it hard to *be* anything else. The profession of almost every man, even the artist, begins with hypocrisy, as he imitates from the outside, copies what is effective."[1] And the philosopher George Santayana (1863–1952) adds that "every one who is sure of his mind, or proud of his office, or anxious about his duty assumes a tragic mask. He deputes it to be himself and transfers to it almost all his vanity."[2]

But role performance has a positive side, too—and it might just be unavoidable. When Jack Donaghy kisses up to Don Geiss on the golf course—because that's what executives do to their bosses in corporate America—we don't fault Jack for not exploring the Platonic forms. When Jenna Maroney feigns injury on the job so she can get her coworkers' sympathy, we laugh at what Nietzsche calls "hypocrisy" (Jenna's the first to complain if Tracy gets more attention than she does). When Kenneth shows too much pride in his NBC rank by handling his beloved page jacket with the material reverence of an American flag—folding it in the official military-triangular arrangement—we also see what Santayana saw: a vanity (perhaps in Kenneth's rising above the social conditions of his birth in

Stone Mountain) and a tragic nature (perhaps in that he will never rise above this position, or that he is so proud of it at all). Similarly, when Liz stays up all night in the writers' room or lacks free time to do her laundry, forcing her to wear a swimsuit instead of underwear, we know it's because she's "anxious about [her] duty" at *TGS*.

But we don't despair in the face of such role performance. On the contrary, we revel in it. Liz's faults make her character more real to us, just as they do for most of the other characters on *30 Rock*. And we love her (and them) for it.[3] We *enjoy* seeing the performances that philosophers have often criticized, perhaps because we see ourselves in these performances. Are we wrong to do so?

Playing Around

Are the *30 Rock* characters ultimately lying to themselves by putting too much emphasis on the roles they perform at work? In *Being and Nothingness*, Jean-Paul Sartre (1905–1980) uses the term "bad faith"—which is a "lie to oneself"—to describe an individual blinded by the rote performance of a particular social role. If you're too focused on a particular social performance, the actions of that position affect you, simplifying and limiting the possibilities open to you. Ironically, as Sartre points out, we *want* to be limited in this way. The human condition is one of radical freedom: we can choose to be anything we want to be, and to do anything we want to do. Because this freedom is terrifying, robbing us of all concrete guidance in how to live our lives, we retreat into the roles available to us. Rather than acknowledging my freedom, I adopt the role of the student, the parent, the professor, the corporate executive, or the page. Existing in these roles gives me a sense of how I ought to be, and what I ought to do. In limiting my possibilities by pretending that I *really am* just a role (or a set of roles), I soften the hard edge of existence: who I am is decided for me, and I can simply go along with what my role demands.

In one of a series of examples, Sartre describes a waiter whose daily performance comes off as forced, putting him in "bad faith":

> His movement is quick and forward, a little too precise, a little too rapid. He comes toward the patrons with a step a little too quick. He bends forward a little too eagerly; his voice, his eyes express an interest a little too solicitous for the order of the customer. Finally there he returns, trying to imitate in his walk the flexible stiffness of some kind of automaton. . . . All his behavior seems to us a game. . . . [H]e is playing at *being* a waiter in a café. There is nothing there to surprise us.[4]

If Kenneth didn't spring to mind while reading this, you should read it again. Kenneth seems, at least initially, to be in bad faith as much as anyone can be. He's a little *too* eager in executing the office of the page. This eagerness is both what we love about Kenneth and what makes him—yes, I'll say it—a little creepy.

But Kenneth has an advantage over Sartre's waiter. If, like me, you've seen every episode of *30 Rock*, then you've accumulated hours of info on Kenneth. We empathize with him, and if he's a little "too precise," "too quick," or "too solicitous" in getting Tracy Jordan some nachos from Yankee Stadium, or a rare fish from Chinatown, we give our favorite Stone Mountain–raised NBC page the benefit of the doubt. But should we? Does Kenneth move past being a molded, repetitious facsimile? Has he run away from the freedom of the human condition into the warm and loving arms of the NBC page program?

Sartre warns that playing a role, while providing some comfort, also makes demands on what we do and who we are. When working, I play a role (and it really doesn't matter what job I have). My performance as a page, a waiter, or a *TGS* writer is merely a "representation" for "others and for myself, which means that I can be he only in *representation*."[5] Human beings are always more than the roles they perform, even when we don't want to be (this is what Sartre calls our "transcendence"—we're always more than any particular mask we wear). "I can not be he, I can only play at being him; that is, imagine to myself that I am he."[6] But as Sartre notes, we take on our jobs with fervor—reducing ourselves to our immediate role performance—because "the public demands [that] of [us]." "A grocer who dreams is offensive to the buyer, because such a grocer is not wholly a grocer."[7]

We don't want a grocer who wishes he were elsewhere. We want him worrying about the quality of our peaches and potatoes. In this respect, we don't want *others* to have the radical freedom that characterizes the human condition, either. We want people to be the roles they occupy, if only because these roles provide us with a guide for how to behave when we interact with others. In responding to others, my responsibility for choosing how to act is removed by pretending that my responses are already predetermined by the roles we all occupy in social space. Jenna seems to understand this as much as anyone could. We can imagine her saying something like this: "Kenneth is a *page*, I'm a superstar. We all know superstars are supposed to abuse the page. That's just the way the world is."

Of course, this *isn't* the way the world is—unless we're in bad faith. The superstar is just as much a role as is the page. For Sartre, we're radically free to have any identity we want. The roles we occupy become excuses for us to shirk our responsibility to make our own decisions.

Performing to Death

We as viewers are buyers—consumers watching what the corporate network produces. We pay with our money and with our time. We want quality returns on that investment, and a page with dreams pays dividends in spades, like Don Quixote with a navy-blue jacket. But rather than dreaming of immediate retirement on a far-off sunny beach, Kenneth has dreams that reinforce the institutions he works for—American television and NBC. While cleaning the NBC news anchor Brian Williams's office with Jack Donaghy, Kenneth puts his dreams in perspective for us:

> Do you know why I put up with this pitiful job, Mr. Donaghy? Why I fetch these folks' lunches, and clean up their barfs? Because they make television. And more than jazz or musical theater or morbid obesity, television is the true American art form. Think of all the shared experiences television has provided for us: from the moon landing to *The Golden Girls* finale, from Walter Cronkite denouncing Vietnam to Oprah pulling that trash bag of fat out in a wagon; from the glory and pageantry of the summer Olympics to the less-fun winter Olympics. So, please, don't tell me I don't have a dream, sir. I am living my dream. ["The Head and the Hair"]

It's hard to think that Kenneth performs his job merely as a staged ceremony when he believes so deeply in the ceremony itself. But that's the way bad faith works. To understand the power of our desire to be defined by our roles—to be reduced to a tidy set of traits, and hence to avoid confronting our freedom—Kenneth's emotional defense of the life of the page is indispensable. Kenneth *believes* in what he does. He's convinced that it constitutes who he is, and in this conviction, all recognition of humanity's radical freedom is lost. (Kenneth's television-affirming, pseudo-patriotic monologue is interrupted, and its semi-ironic pathos undercut, by a pizza falling from the ceiling—presumably somehow put there by anchor and partier Brian Williams. It's almost as though Brian Williams wants to wake Kenneth up from his bad faith!)

How loyal is Kenneth in his love for television? A few episodes earlier we see him on the *Conan* set telling about his life post-television.

> Kenneth: Well, I got started in the NBC page program, and before you know it I'm making hit movies with my good friend and roommate, Zach Braff. [*mimes drinking from the mug and smiling at imaginary Conan*] What? Who told you that? Well, yes, I do know how to clog. But I don't think anybody wants to see me do that. [*looks to fake audience*] You do? Really? Okay . . . [*starts clogging on Conan's set*]
>
> [*The real Conan O'Brien enters and walks by on the stage.*]
>
> Conan: You're a weird guy, Kenneth. ["Tracy Does Conan"]

Kenneth's moviemaking and clogging fantasy is probably just a temporary dalliance. Besides, Kenneth's loyalty to television is upheld by the fact that he successfully plugs NBC three times during the short imaginary interview: supporting Conan and his show, the NBC page program, and NBC product Zach Braff, star of *Scrubs*.

But where is the real Kenneth? The one who's *not* performing? Even his moral sensibilities are totally enmeshed with his role as a page. When there isn't enough flu vaccine for everyone in the studio, Kenneth declares that it would be his "honor to die at my post." He will literally die for the corporation.

And performing to death isn't unique to Kenneth. Most every employee on *30 Rock* is willing to sacrifice life and body for the good of NBC. Starting at the top, Don Geiss confides to Jack Donaghy that because of work-related stress he has had some near-death experiences: "Take care of yourself, Jack. I've technically died twice." And Geiss's family life suffers too, as he admits to Jack that he intends to spend more time with his family, but work has not allowed it. Geiss then ups the ante by saying he even has a secret family that he also has not been able to see because of work. In the same episode, Jack Donaghy endures heart problems and simultaneously risks death by competing in athletic events to beat out Devon Banks for Geiss's CEO position. Jack rhetorically asks Don Geiss's little granddaughter Caitlin, "Is it really worth it, I wonder. I mean, I almost let a man die today and for what? A bigger office? More money?"

If it's offensive for a grocer to be anything but a grocer, is it offensive for Jack to be anything more than we expect him to be? Could we tolerate the younger version of Jack—the one that interned for Ted Kennedy, for example? Probably not. Could we tolerate a Kenneth who disdained television? We wouldn't even recognize him. Bad faith, it seems, is simply a part of the way we understand ourselves and each other. We perform our selves, and the only thing behind the performance is a freedom we find terrifying.

Brass Balls: Performing Gender

It's no surprise that Alec Baldwin plays the role of the company man hell-bent on motivating others in their workplace performance. Tina Fey wrote Jack Donaghy (motto: "Capitalism is my religion") with Baldwin in mind. And after watching the film version of David Mamet's *Glengarry Glen Ross* (1992) in which Mamet wrote the role of Blake for Baldwin (a role *not* in the Pulitzer Prize–winning play), one can see why Fey cast Bladwin in the role of Donaghy. In the *30 Rock* episode "Six Sigma Retreat," Liz tells Jack to "always be talking" when they are trying to complete a team-building block-construction contest together. This is an allusion to Baldwin's *Glengarry Glen Ross* character, one of the bosses at a shady real estate company, who gives an intense, intimidating, rousing speech instructing the company salesmen to "always be closing." In Blake's speech, which I would recommend looking up on youtube.com to experience its full performed effect, we see a rougher, more ragged, ruthless Jack Donaghy. Blake is Jack Donaghy in leaner, angrier, precorporate times:

> A-B-C. A—always, B—be, C—closing. Always be closing! Always be closing! . . .
>
> You see this watch? You see this watch? . . . That watch cost more than your car. I made $970,000 last year. How much you make? You see, pal, that's who I am. And you're nothing. Nice guy? I don't give a shit. Good father? Fuck you—go home and play with your kids!! You wanna work here? Close!

Blake's identity as an individual, his performance of self, is directly linked to the amount of money he makes. "Who he is" is his income.

And to be even more specific, in an office full of men, it's Blake's *masculine* identity on full display. Later in the speech, Blake literally pulls out a pair of brass balls and tells the salesmen—and all of them are men—that these are what they need in order to successfully sell real estate. While both Alec Baldwin characters are capitalists and company men, Jack Donaghy proudly navigates the massive corporate structure. In the same "Six Sigma Retreat" episode, Jack psyches himself up in the mirror before giving a speech to GE's corporate elite. He tells himself, "Well, buddy, here we come. Bases loaded, bottom of the ninth, are you gonna step up? Oh, yeah! Because it's winning time, you magnificent son of a bitch! You go in there and show them! Make mommy proud of her big boy because he's the best." Apart from the comic mommy bit, Jack's speech could be Blake's from Mamet's film, but then Jack adds a string of corporate slogans: "Just do it! Is it in you? I'm lovin' it!" With Nike, Gatorade, and McDonald's to inspire him, Jack knows he's safe. He *is* the corporation—every stinking man-inch of it.

With all this talk of brass balls and outpositioning other men in corporate America, we become eyewitnesses to the performance of gender. Judith Butler, a leading voice in philosophy and gender studies, uses the term "performativity" to describe how we approach our own gendering on a day-to-day basis: a "repeated set of actions" that we have learned through social conditioning and continue to practice without thinking. Much like a script, you and I follow and rehearse the identity we choose. Our identities, including our gender (the way you perform your form of masculinity or femininity), are not ingrained in us, but *chosen*.

Historically, corporate America has upheld the family ethos. Capitalism has found that the nuclear family results in productive workers and a successful company. For that reason, Don Geiss tells Jack he should look for a wife, and Jack constantly encourages Liz Lemon's dating life. Given the family ethos, it seems strange that Jack Donaghy has some sort of crush on Don Geiss. Just think of the time he sings "Simply the Best" all alone in front of the portrait of Geiss he himself painted. In the same episode, Jack hopes to golf with Geiss, saying he wants "an intense four-hour foursome with three other men" on the course. There's also an ongoing man-love between Jack and Dick Cheney. At one point we see Jack and Dick together at the Pentagon. Two military men embrace lovingly in the background, and Jack says to Dick, "Please be gentle," then quickly takes off Cheney's jacket. Later in the Valentine's Day episode, Jack admits that he "may have sodomized our former vice president while under the influence of some weapons-grade narcotics."

The nontraditional connection between corporate power and homosexuality continues as Jack says about his rival: "Devon Banks is gay. He's more powerful than I thought." Sometimes, though, *30 Rock* shows us not homosexuality but homosociality: the old-fashioned enjoyment of being in the company of men, but not necessarily sexually. Floyd, Liz's boyfriend before he moves off to Cleveland, admits his feelings for Jack, and Jack reciprocates. This "bromance" continues until Liz tells Jack to leave her man alone. Jack tells Liz: "Lemon, you are the third wheel. . . . It's really quite simple. Men seek out the company of other men that they admire and want to be like. Floyd is me twenty years ago. I'm Don Geiss thirty years ago. Twenty years from now, Floyd will be me, I'll be Don Geiss, and Don Geiss will be dead." It's one big corporate cycle, like a family tree but with fathers and sons born in the boardroom.

Sometimes turning bad faith into good can come with a moment of unexpected sincerity, when the role you customarily play is altered. In explaining patterns of bad faith, Sartre's first example is of a "woman who has consented to go out with a particular man for the first time."[8] Because the man is interested in her on different levels, socially and sexually, he takes her hand, "changing the situation by calling for an immediate decision."[9] The woman chooses to lie to herself (bad faith) and "postpone the moment of decision as long as possible"—withdraw her hand or leave it there.[10] But, Sartre continues, she may not notice the hand because "at this moment" she is "all intellect": mentally drawing "her companion up to the most lofty regions of sentimental speculation."[11] But in an episode on *30 Rock*, in a moment of absolute sincerity, of *good* faith, Jenna is true to herself and to the realities of the world around her and her abilities. This moment of authenticity happens at the birthday party for the last remaining royal Hapsburg of the Austro-Hungarian Empire played by Paul Reubens. After Liz asks Jenna, "Wait, you're actually considering [rendezvousing with the duke]?" Jenna replies:

Of course I'm considering it. You know I've always reminded myself of Grace Kelly. I'm not going to be gorgeous forever. Who knows how long this show will last, and I have no other skills whatsoever. I need to find someone who can take care of me. . . . I'm an actress, Liz. It would be my greatest role of all time!" ["Black Tie"]

Sartre talks about the terror women would feel if they realized consciously they were being used for their bodies. Jenna, however, doesn't mind. She's open in her self-serving ways, and seems happy to play the roles she's given (even when they don't involve reprising Janis Joplin).

Final Act

The actors on *30 Rock* play their parts beautifully. But the characters—Kenneth, Liz, Jack, Tracy, Jenna, and everyone else—also play their parts with conviction and consistency. The only difference between the two, it seems, is that the actors on *30 Rock* know they are performing. Tina Fey knows she's not Liz Lemon; Alec Baldwin knows he's not Jack Donaghy. But Kenneth doesn't know he's not a page. Jack would have a heart attack if we told him he wasn't *really* a corporate lackey. We would like to think we're better than this. But in truth we spend our lives much as they do: performing roles that help us to ignore the near-infinite range of possibilities open to us. How's that for a feel-good ending?

NOTES

1. Friedrich Nietzsche, *Human, All Too Human*, translated by Marion Faber (Lincoln: University of Nebraska Press, 1984), 51.

2. George Santayana, *Soliloquies in England and Later Soliloquies* (New York: Charles Scribner's Sons, 1922), 133–134. Credit to Marvin Carlson for bringing the Nietzsche and Santayana quotes to my attention in *Performance* (London and New York: Routledge, 1996), 42–43. Carlson's book is a great primer on many aspects of performance studies.

3. I would exclude Jenna from ever being fully human or likable. Jenna is likable for two moments out of the three seasons so far: "Me Want Food," and "Muffin Top." Right? I will redeem Jenna at the end of this essay if you happen to be a Jenna fan.

4. Jean-Paul Sartre, *Being and Nothingness*, translated by Hazel E. Barnes (New York: Philosophical Library, 1956), 48.

5. Ibid., 60.

6. Ibid.

7. Ibid.

8. Ibid., 55.

9. Ibid.

10. Ibid.

11. Ibid., 56.

APPENDIX 1

Frank's Hat Store

1. Ninja Expert
2. Done Deal
3. Extra Sausage
4. Mind the Gap
5. Double Cheese
6. Arcade Champ
7. Hand Held
8. Joystick Master
9. Bigfoot Expert
10. Over Easy
11. E.S.P. Tutor
12. Kung Fu Beech
13. Rods
14. Karate Sluts
15. Beef N Bean
16. Smells
17. Extra Cheese
18. 1,000,000 Points
19. UFO Cop
20. Cool as Ice
21. Time Travel Agent
22. Liz Rocks
23. Mash Potatos
24. Beef Ravioli
25. Atomic Super Kick
26. Mystery Solver
27. Bahama Trapezoid
28. Alabama Legsweep
29. Alien Knight Force
30. Coin-Operated
31. Kill Screen
32. Ready
33. Field Hockey Coach
34. Balls
35. And
36. Lips
37. Half Centaur
38. Karate Prom
39. Olé
40. Right Boot
41. Got It
42. Handy Man
43. Beer
44. Burrito
45. Power Tool
46. Atlantas Lifeguard
47. Harvard [on a top hat]
48. Kayfabe
49. Shower Scene
50. Ho Ho Horny [Santa trucker hat]
51. Or
52. Exactly
53. Trap Do r

54. Rescue Team
55. Speling Expirt
56. Sumo Dog
57. Slo-Bot
58. Former Cyclops
59. Horny
60. Alien Abductee
61. Role Model
62. Foley Artist
63. Bronx Golf Club
64. Night Chicks
65. Pinball Mechanic
66. Phase 3
67. Feelin' It
68. Emotional Friend
69. Incompl te
70. Two Fare Zone
71. Reverse Pendulum
72. Hair Drapes
73. Laser Disc
74. Game Changer
75. Constant Craving
76. Space Gravy
77. Flowers
78. Fedora [with a purple feather]
79. Crop Octagon
80. Mute Button
81. Disco Fries
82. Long Pips
83. Spaceship Owner
84. Not Guilty
85. Wet to Activate
86. Seemiller Grip
87. Busway
88. Scanner
89. Shark Cop
90. Because
91. Sdrawkcab
92. First Class
93. Teenage Grandpa
94. PG-25
95. Karate Hockey
96. Soccer
97. In Training
98. Wide and Tight
99. Delete
100. Night Beast

APPENDIX 2

The Wisdom of the Page:
Meet Kenneth Ellen Parcell

- Kenneth's a remarkably good poker player, though he has been known to get confused about the rules.
- Kenneth's middle name is Ellen.
- Kenneth's Meyers-Briggs psychological testing shows a rare combination of extroverted, intuitive, and aggressive.
- Kenneth believes that life is for the living. It's for taking risks, and biting off more than you can chew.
- Kenneth fantasizes about making movies with his "good friend" Zach Braff.
- Kenneth's mother always told him that even when things seem bad, there's someone else who's having a worse day. Like being stung by a bee or getting a splinter or being chained to a wall in someone's sex dungeon. ("The Baby Show")
- Kenneth's mother is his best friend.
- Kenneth disrespected Ridikolous once by refusing to let him into Tracy's party. As Kenneth explained. "Mr. Jordan himself said, 'Don't let no one in who's not on the list, 'cause this mess is gonna get raw like sushi.' So, haters to the left." ("The Source Awards")
- Kenneth grew up on a pig farm, where he fattened up and grew to love his pigs, only to have his uncles slit their throats.
- Kenneth's mother had a boyfriend named Ron. He moved in when Kenneth's dad's heart just "up and gave out" from an unhealthy diet.
- Kenneth inherited Jack's Cookie Jar collection.

- Kenneth learned at least one great put-down from Ron: the classic "smooth move, ex-lax."
- Kenneth on cookie jars: "Well, I guess I've never thought about it that much. We had a nice one back home in Georgia. Had a bear on it. I remember when my mom's friend Ron would come over. They'd go into the bedroom to sort out their paperwork, and I'd just go ahead and stare at that cookie jar. It was almost as if I took every problem that I ever had and I put it inside that cookie jar. And I sealed it up so tight that nothing would ever, ever, ever get out. So, I guess to answer your question, I'd give cookie jars about a 'B.'" ("The Collection")
- Kenneth gets sad thinking about people with too many problems to be contained by a cookie jar.
- According to Kenneth's Bible, 1999 will be in seven years.
- Kenneth is "a stupid country bumpkin with great skin and soft hands," according to his Uncle Butch. ("Somebody to Love")
- Kenneth, like all of the Parcell clan, is "neither wealthy nor circumcised." ("Somebody to Love") Kenneth is not particularly good at coaching inner-city children in Little League, though he sure does try.
- Kenneth on Christmas: "Well, that's not the Christmas spirit. Christmas is about gratitude and togetherness. Sitting with friends and family around a crackling fire, waiting for the owl meat to cook. Sometimes I don't think you people understand Christmas at all." ("Ludachristmas")
- Kenneth was addicted to Coke in his "Wall Street Days."
- Kenneth is confused about the rules of the game "Murder" (as well as the rules of poker).
- Kenneth on hot drinks: "I don't drink coffee, sir. I don't drink hot liquids of any kind. That's the Devil's temperature." ("Episode 210")
- Kenneth on coffee, after drinking it: "I love how it makes me feel. It's like my heart is trying to hug my brain. You know what we've never done, Grizz? Fight each other!" ("Episode 210")

- Kenneth on coffee, reflecting on his experience: "It's not just the coffee. I also went to a PG-13 movie. I bought a pair of sunglasses. I tried a Jewish doughnut. I'd always been told that New York was the twenty-first-century city of Sodom. And look what's happened. I've become one of them. I've been sodomized." ("Episode 210")
- Kenneth speaks German. After all, "If you're not reading the Bible in German you're not getting the real *versteckte Bedeutung* of it." ("Episode 210")
- Kenneth made two promises to his mother before moving to New York: "One, if I found any Mackenzies living up here I would kill them. And two, I would not let this city change me." ("Episode 210")
- Kenneth's uncle used to drink from the air conditioner.
- Kenneth's cousin Stephen came out after attending music college.
- Kenneth on lying: "The weight of a lie makes your soul so heavy that you can't raise up to Heaven. And you don't look good in jeans from behind." ("MILF Island")
- Kenneth on voting in a democracy: "I don't vote Republican or Democrat. Choosing is a sin, so I always just write in the Lord's name." ("Subway Hero") According to Jack, these votes count as Republican.
- Kenneth doesn't believe in drinking, gambling, or freeway driving.
- Kenneth calls alcohol "Hill People Milk," which he's been drinking since he was a baby.
- Three of Kenneth's nine siblings were adopted . . . and someday, he's going to find them.
- Kenneth on hypothetical situations: "I don't believe in hypothetical situations. . . . That's like lying to your brain." ("Believe in the Stars")
- Kenneth loves two things in this world: everybody and television.
- Kenneth knows that stealing from the poor, helpless cable company is just wrong.

- Kenneth finds Spongebob Squarepants completely terrifying.
- The last time Kenneth was blindfolded was when he had to play the piano at that weird masquerade party. ("The One with the Cast of 'Night Court'")
- Kenneth on childhood disobedience: "Sometimes, kids act out when there's a big change. I know I was a handful when my family moved from our farmhouse to that militia camp in the woods." ("Gavin Volure")
- Kenneth loves helping people less fortunate than he is. He finds these people with the help of some Nigerians on the Internet.
- The traditional burial of a Parcell man involves being wrapped in a Confederate flag, fried, and fed to dogs.
- Uncle Harlan Parcell was known to drink in excess (not to mention the wistful jug blowing).
- Kenneth is the safest place in 30 Rockefeller Center.
- Kenneth has a skull press for pickling squirrel meat.
- If Kenneth were in charge, all menstruating women would be sent home immediately.
- Kenneth is farm strong and heart strong.
- Kenneth practices phrenology, believing that the shape of the skull can tell us what kind of person someone is.
- Kenneth has acute ventriculitis, but his heart also skips a beat for one of the *TGS* dancers.
- Kenneth is allergic to strawberries. If he eats one, his throat "shuts up faster than a girl in math class." ("The Ones")
- Kenneth calls his harmonica his mouth radio.
- Kenneth's real name might be Dick Whitman.
- Kenneth on a traumatic memory: "Well as a child I had a prized pig that I thought was my best friend. But then one day I picked up one of her piglets, she went crazy. She bit off my nut sack that I kept tied around my belt to feed squirrels." ("The Natural Order")
- Kenneth loves S&M magazines (that's his abbreviation for "super and magical").

- Kenneth's favorite subject was science, especially the Old Testament.
- Kenneth believes that the Parcell name is synonymous with honesty.
- Kenneth always works more than sixteen hours.
- Kenneth learned that bonus means extra from game shows.
- Kenneth volunteers for Pants for Zoo Animals and Big Brother. "This big brother isn't affiliated with the mentoring program. It's an organization that secretly watches people and makes sure they're behaving properly." ("Into the Crevasse")
- Kenneth on growing up in Stone Mountain, Georgia: "I grew up on a pig farm, sir, where even the birds that cleaned out teeth were workers not pets. I never even had a dog because as my mom would say, 'You can't eat love.' And as my mom's friend Ron would say, 'The donkey died, you're the donkey now Kenneth.'" ("Into the Crevasse")
- Kenneth on the history of the Parcell clan: "When the Parcells first came to America they lived in a town called Sexcriminalboat. Do you think that's Cherokee?" ("Stone Mountain")
- Kenneth on what makes him laugh: "Two hobos sharing a bean, lady airline pilots. I remember growing up in Stone Mountain, my whole family would go down to the Chuckle Hut . . . See, the chuckle is the part of the pig between the tail and the anus, but at night the Chuckle Hut becomes the Laugh Factory and that's a comedy club." ("Stone Mountain")
- Kenneth refers to bed bugs as chew daddies, Ozark kisses, and the woodsmen's companion.
- Kenneth comes from Stone Mountain, where the mayor was a horse with bed bugs.
- Kenneth sleeps in the one pair of shoes he owns.
- Kenneth observes backwards day.

- Sometimes, Kenneth feels about as useless as a Momma's college degree.
- Kenneth doesn't like it when people say he's been alive forever.
- Kenneth can unhinge his pelvis.
- Kenneth learned his airport codes in high school.
- Kenneth thinks "irritated" is a swear word.
- Kenneth has widdled teeth.
- Kenneth might be over forty. (He's affected by low tones that only those over forty can hear.)
- Kenneth advocates summer shorts for the pages at NBC.
- Kenneth is not alone in blaming Liz Lemon for winter.

CONTRIBUTORS

Cast Members of *30 Rock and Philosophy*

Robert Arp is a philosopher who now builds ontologies for the U.S. Air Force. He edited *South Park and Philosophy*, coedited *Batman and Philosophy*, and also does work in philosophy of biology. Like Tracy Jordan, he wants to live every week like it's Shark Week.

Adam Barkman is assistant professor of Philosophy at Redeemer University College. He is the author of *C. S. Lewis and Philosophy as a Way of Life* and *Through Common Things* and is the coeditor of *Manga and Philosophy*. He has published more than thirty articles, many of which have to do with philosophy and popular culture. And if he ever gets called for jury duty, he's going dressed as Han Solo.

Ashley Barkman is sometimes a prof, recently a mom of two, and always a wife of one. Her latest publications include articles in *Manga and Philosophy* and *Mad Men and Philosophy*. She finds it unfortunate that her throat shuts up like a girl in math class when writing blurbs.

Michael Da Silva is a law student at the University of Toronto. He is vice president of the Canadian Society of Christian

Philosophers and a contributor to *Arrested Development and Philosophy*.

Kevin S. Decker is an assistant professor of Philosophy at Eastern Washington University. He's the coeditor of *Star Wars and Philosophy* and *Star Trek and Philosophy* (both with Jason T. Eberl), and *Terminator and Philosophy* (with Richard Brown). He has written on philosophical topics in popular culture such as James Bond, the films of Stanley Kubrick, *The Colbert Report*, and *Transformers*. And this means he's a dealbreaker, ladies.

P. Sue Dohnimm is only as real as your favorite *30 Rock* character.

Melina Found is currently completing her Bachelor of Arts and Sciences in Studio Art and Zoology at the University of Guelph. She is competing with Michael Da Silva to head the General Electric Gold Boots Production Division.

Jeffrey A. Hinzmann (or "Jeff" to his friends and enemies) is a graduate student at the University of South Florida. His interests include Richard Rorty's critique of, and place in, the history of analytic philosophy, philosophy of psychology, and philosophy of music. This is his first publication and he is excited thinking of all the people he can bore to death talking about it. He spends his free time wondering where his free time went and trying to find Jenna's vacation home in nearby Clearwater, Florida.

Nicolas Michaud teaches philosophy at the University of North Florida and the Art Institute of Jacksonville. His story is a sad one, beginning with his impoverished childhood in which he was relegated to going to school in an old school-marm's attic with only Chippy the mouse as his friend. Nick eventually pulled himself up by the bootstraps and taught himself advanced calculus for space flight, 230 different languages, including the ability to communicate solely by blinking in Morse code, and the martial art known as NoKeeJu, which is taught entirely through correspondence course via e-mail. Nick can now be found embedded in the bureaucracy of his chosen institutions, doing nothing of any use to anyone.

Marc E. Shaw is an assistant professor of theater arts at Hartwick College. His recent publications include two chapters in anthologies: one about Harold Pinter's *The Dumb Waiter* and another about the images of masculinity in Neil LaBute's plays. Although Shaw is not a lupine Jew, his spooky/scary dream is to have his own "Werewolf Bar Mitzvah."

Tyler Shores is a graduate student in English at Oxford. He received his B.A. from the University of California, Berkeley, where he created and for six semesters taught a course on the Simpsons and philosophy (inspired by William Irwin's book of the same name). Tyler has contributed to *Heroes and Philosophy*, *Alice in Wonderland and Philosophy*, and *Arrested Development and Philosophy*. He has also previously worked at Google and the Authors@Google lecture series. He aspires to someday be a *TGS* writer, because he feels he has a lot on his mindgrapes that should be put down on paper.

Andrew Terjesen is currently a visiting assistant professor of philosophy at Rhodes College in Memphis, Tennessee. He has previously taught at Washington and Lee University and Austin College. Andrew's interests recently have become focused on issues in business ethics, especially with regard to the relationship between morality and capitalism and the effects of corporate structures on ethical decision making. In addition, he enjoys writing essays that explore the philosophical issues in popular culture and has contributed essays to such Pop Culture and Philosophy volumes as *The Office and Philosophy* and *Iron*

Man and Philosophy (which has an essay on the ethics of wealth distribution). Andrew desperately wants to be the ghost writer on the sequel to Jack Donaghy's *Jack Attack*, tentatively titled "Jack Off: The Art of Aggression in Business Vacations."

J. Jeremy Wisnewski has edited *Family Guy and Philosophy*, *The Office and Philosophy*, and *Arrested Development and Philosophy* (with Kristopher Philips). He has also written *Wittgenstein and Ethical Inquiry*, *The Politics of Agency*, and *The Ethics of Torture*. He is contemplating giving up writing, though, to take up full-time work as a page for NBC.

Dan Yim is a college professor living in Minneapolis, Minnesota. He likes writing about early modern philosophy, and his articles have appeared in *Locke Studies* and the *British Journal for the History of Philosophy*. He relaxes by taking long walks along peaceful lake shores while he imagines nightmarishly awkward scenarios for Liz Lemon's dating life. Good times . . .

INDEX

Shinehardt Wig Company Filing System

femininity
  third-wave feminism and, 90
  workaholism and, 18, 20
  See also third-wave feminism
feminism. *See* third-wave
  feminism
"fetishism of commodities,"
  109–111, 112
Fey, Tina, 176, 206. *See also*
  Lemon, Liz
first-person perspective, 103
Fisher, Carrie, 176
Floyd, 53, 93–94
  identity and, 205
  sexuality and, 83
  social constructivism and,
    174–176, 184–185
  workaholism and, 20, 22
Frankfurt School, 24–25
free will, 25
French, Peter, 118–120, 130,
  131–133
Freud, Sigmund
  Frankfurt School and, 25
  sexuality and, 78–79
  time and self, 171
  on work and love, 22–23
friendship, 28–30
  goodwill and, 40–42
  mutual pleasure and, 34–40
  utility and, 31–34, 37, 39

Geiss, Don
  corporate management and,
    117, 118, 119, 121, 126
  corporations as persons and,
    131–132, 137
  identity and, 201–202, 204,
    205

  sexuality and, 77, 83
Geiss, Kathy
  corporate management
    and, 118
  sexuality and, 77
  virtue and, 46
gender
  identity and, 202–206
  sexuality and, 82, 87–88
General Electric (GE), 39, 203
  corporate management and,
    114–129
  corporations as persons
    and, 132
  libertarianism and
    communitarianism, 143
genetics, sexuality and, 81
Girlie Show, The (TGS), 17, 36
Glengarry Glen Ross (film),
  202–203
gods/God, virtue and, 52–53
goodwill, friendship and, 40–42
Greece (ancient), 75–76
Green, Milton, 106
Greenzo, 116
Grizz
  friendship and, 30–32
  race and, 68, 71

Habermas, Jürgen, 112
Hacking, Ian, 177–178, 182
happiness
  delusion and, 150, 160
  virtue and, 45–46
Haslanger, Sally, 177
"having it all"
  delusion and, 153–155
  third-wave feminism and,
    91, 98